STRONG MEDICINE

STRONG MEDICINE

■ ■ ■ ■

CREATING INCENTIVES FOR PHARMACEUTICAL

RESEARCH ON NEGLECTED DISEASES

Michael Kremer and
Rachel Glennerster

*Published with the generous support
of the Brookings Institution
and the Center for Global Development*

PRINCETON UNIVERSITY PRESS
Princeton and Oxford

Published by Princeton University Press, 41 William Street,
Princeton, New Jersey 08540

In the United Kingdom: Princeton University Press, 3 Market Place,
Woodstock, Oxfordshire OX20 1SY

LIBRARY OF CONGRESS CATALOGING-IN-PUBLICATION DATA
Kremer, Michael, 1964–
Strong medicine : creating incentives for pharmaceutical research on neglected diseases /
Michael Kremer and Rachel Glennerster.
p.   cm.
Includes bibliographical references and index.
ISBN 0-691-12113-3 (cl : alk. paper)
1. Pharmacy—Research—Economic aspects—Developing countries.
2. Drugs—Research—Economic aspects—Developing countries.
3. Vaccines—Research—Economic aspects—Developing countries.
I. Glennerster, Rachel. II. Title.
RS122.K74 2004
362.17′82′091724—dc22   2004050384

British Library Cataloging-in-Publication Data is available

This book has been composed in Sabon and Copperplate 29

Printed on acid-free paper. ∞

pup.princeton.edu

Printed in the United States of America

1   3   5   7   9   10   8   6   4   2

To our parents

CONTENTS

FOREWORD

In this book, Michael Kremer and Rachel Glennerster set out an idea that is winning support from across the political spectrum and has the potential to save millions of lives throughout the developing world. The simple but powerful idea is that if governments or private foundations were to commit in advance to purchase vaccines for diseases like malaria, this would stimulate R&D into these vaccines. Moreover, once the vaccines were developed, they could be made available at little or no cost to those who needed them. This approach represents economics at its best—applying market-based incentives to address the needs of the poorest people in the world.

Back in 1998 with support from the Brookings Institution, where he is a senior fellow, Michael Kremer published an academic paper explaining how government purchases of patents could reward innovation while making sure the technology was freely available to all once it was developed. This might have remained simply an interesting paper in an academic journal, except that Michael was also involved in research in rural Kenya, where he was exposed firsthand to the enormous human cost of diseases like malaria and HIV/AIDS. Why was there so little research on these deadly diseases? Couldn't a mechanism similar to a patent buyout both stimulate R&D into vaccines and make the eventual vaccine available at low cost to those who needed it?

Michael set to work to explore the theoretical and practical dimensions of a vaccine commitment and make the case for the idea (including in Kremer 2001a, 2001b). Partly as a result, there has been growing political support for a vaccine commitment. A version of such a commitment was backed by Lawrence Summers when he was Treasury Secretary and was included in the final Clinton tax bill (although this was never passed). Bills providing for some form of vaccine commitment have also been sponsored by influential congressional leaders including Bill Frist, Nancy Pelosi, and John Kerry. The concept has been further shaped and made more concrete in the last year, by a distinguished and independent working group set up at the request of the Bill & Melinda Gates Foundation by the Center for Global Development's Global Health Policy Research Network. The working group brings together experts on vaccine development, contract law, the economics of the pharmaceutical industry, and other fields to forge a proposal mindful of, and sensitive to, the practical realities of implementation. Over the last year this group, co-chaired by Michael, Ruth Levine, Senior Fellow at the Center for Global Development, and Alice Albright, Chief Financial Officer of the Vaccine Fund, has examined issues such as what diseases and products should be the initial focus of a commitment, what is the appropriate scale of incentives, and how a commitment can be made credible and legally binding. This book has benefited from the resulting insights, while reflecting the views of the authors. The working group's report, draft legal contracts, and analytical tools for evaluating the appropriate size of commitment complement the exposition in this book.

Michael Kremer and Rachel Glennerster have brought their policy experience and knowledge of economics to bear to present, in an easily accessible way, a wealth of information on subjects ranging from how health problems differ in developing and advanced economies, to the reasons why there is so little research on vaccines, to the cost-effectiveness of a vaccine commitment. As an example of how economics can be used to analyze and solve important policy problems and improve the lives of some of the poorest in the world, it is an ideal read for those interested in development policy as well as for students interested in the application of economics to policy solutions. Anyone involved in formulating policy on health in developing countries and on promoting R&D in general will find the insights on how a vaccine commitment could be made operational invaluable.

NANCY BIRDSALL
President, *Center for Global Development*

STROBE TALBOTT
President, *Brookings Institution*

ACKNOWLEDGMENTS

This book reflects comments and ideas from many people. In particular, it draws on the deliberations of the Pull Mechanisms Working Group of the Global Health Policy Research Network, a program of the Center for Global Development that is supported by the Bill & Melinda Gates Foundation. We are grateful to the Center for Global Development and the Bill & Melinda Gates Foundation for financial support and to the members and staff of the working group for comments and suggestions. We are particularly grateful to Ruth Levine for her many useful suggestions, as well as for her extensive comments on drafts of this manuscript. We would also like to thank the WHO Commission on Macroeconomics and Health, the Brookings Institution, and the MacArthur Foundation's Network on the Costs of Inequality for their support of our earlier analytical work on financial incentives for R&D on vaccines, on which this book draws. Comments from colleagues from each of these groups were very helpful.

The idea of encouraging R&D by committing to purchase vaccines once they are developed was discussed in WHO (1996a) and was advocated by a coalition of organizations coordinated by the International AIDS Vaccine Initiative at the 1997 Denver G-8 summit. The World Bank AIDS Vaccine Task Force (Rosenhouse 1999; World Bank 2000) explored this idea further. Sachs and Kremer (1999) and Sachs (1999) have advocated the establishment of such pull programs in the popular press.

This report also draws on earlier writing on vaccines, including Batson (1998), Dupuy and Freidel (1990), Mercer Management Consulting (1998), and Milstien and Batson (1994), as well as on the broader academic literature on research incentives, including Guell and Fischbaum (1995), Johnston and Zeckhauser (1991), Lanjouw and Cockburn (2001), Lichtmann (1997), Russell (1998), Scotchmer (1999), Shavell and van Ypserle (1998), and Wright (1983). The section on R&D incentives in tropical agriculture draws heavily on Kremer and Zwane (2003). The discussion of legal issues in chapter 12 is based on Morantz and Sloane (2001).

The conviction that a vaccine purchase commitment could become a practical reality grew out of a conversation with Jeffrey Sachs. Jeff's encouragement, support, and intellectual input were critical in getting this project off the ground. We are grateful to Daron Acemoglu, Philippe Aghion, Martha Ainsworth, Susan Athey, Amir Attaran, Abhijit Banerjee, Amie Batson, Peter Berman, Ernie Berndt, Nancy Birdsall, David Cutler, Sara Ellison, Sarah England, John Gallup, Gargee Ghosh, Carol Graham, Chandresh Harjivan, John Hurvitz, Dean Jamison, Eugene Kandel, Hannah Kettler, Jenny Lanjouw, Sendhil Mullainathan, Ariel Pakes, Ok Pannenborg, Leighton Reid, Sydney Rosen, Andrew Segal, Raj Shah, Scott Stern, Larry Summers, Wendy Taylor, Jean Tirole, Adrian Towse, David Weber, and Georg Weizsäcker for comments and discussions on these issues. Radu Ban, Marcos Chamon, Andrew Francis, Fabia Gumbau, Amar Hamoudi, Jane Kim, Jean Lee, Ben Olken, Anjali Oza, Kathy Paur, Margaret Ronald, Courtney Umberger, Heidi Williams, and Alix Peterson Zwane provided excellent research assistance. We are grateful to Katherine Lynch and Peter Passell for their assistance in editing this book, and to our editors at Princeton University Press, Peter Dougherty and Tim Sullivan.

1. INTRODUCTION

After graduating from college, I spent a year teaching high school in a rural area of western Kenya.[1] Six months into the job, I went to Nairobi to purchase textbooks for the school and run some other errands. When I arrived I felt a bit like a country bumpkin, having been living in a house with mud walls and a thatched roof and suddenly being surrounded by skyscrapers. People in western Kenya had told me that Nairobi, situated at some 5,000 feet in altitude, would be very cold. As someone who was used to Kansas winters, I assumed what constituted "cold" in equatorial Nairobi would not affect me, but I did, indeed, find myself getting chills.

As I made my rounds in Nairobi, I felt very lethargic. I would stop into a restaurant, order food, and then realize I couldn't bring myself to eat. I would leave and, feeling weak, go into another restaurant, order food, and again push it away. The next day I would feel better and wonder why I'd been so sluggish, only to again slip into lethargy and weakness a bit later. This went on for several days.

At one point I needed to make a phone call, and sought out the nearest pay phone, which happened to be in a hospital—actually, one of the best private hospitals in Nairobi. While making the call, I realized I was too weak to walk out and had to see a doctor.

It turned out that an anopheles mosquito had gotten past my mosquito net and bitten me, injecting the infective form of the malaria parasite, known as sporozoites, into my blood. The parasites had

---

[1] The personal experiences related in this Introduction are Michael Kremer's.

moved to my liver, where they changed form and reproduced, giving rise to blood-stage malaria.

As the parasites multiplied, destroying my red blood cells, I began to experience nausea, exhaustion, fever, sweating, and shaking chills. My alternating periods of strength and weakness were characteristic of malaria. If I had been out in the village and not gotten to a doctor, the condition could have led to death through severe anemia, or by stemming blood flow to the brain and other organs.

I checked into the hospital in Nairobi. My memory of what happened thereafter is a blur. I remember waking from strange nightmarish dreams. The type of malaria I had proved resistant to the first-line drug used to fight the disease, but the doctors switched me to alternatives and kept me on them until I recovered. I returned to the village fifteen pounds lighter.

Of course, I was phenomenally lucky to receive first-rate care. Many people in Africa live far from clinics, cannot afford to see a competent doctor, or do not have the money to pay for effective medicine.

I saw this vividly illustrated years later when I returned for a visit to the village where I had lived in Kenya. One of my friends there had malaria. Unlike me, he recognized the symptoms, but he lived several hour's walk from a hospital, and was not much inclined to go there in any case, knowing that patients regularly have to share a bed. The first-line malaria medicine is readily available over-the-counter in Kenya, and costs less than a dollar. But when I arrived, my friend hadn't been medicated because he couldn't afford the pills. While he was unlikely to die from the disease, he was sufficiently sick to be unable to work, and the resulting inability to afford essentials made him even weaker.

Malaria is only one of the diseases that plague low-income countries. Together, malaria, tuberculosis, and the strains of HIV common in Africa kill 5 million people each year. Diseases like schistosomiasis, which many people in higher-income countries have never heard of, also impose a heavy burden on poor countries. Vaccines offer the best hope for conquering these diseases because they are relatively easy to deliver, even in countries with weak health-care infrastructure. Yet research on vaccines for diseases that primarily affect low-income countries remains minimal.

In this book we examine the reasons for this lack of research and propose that foreign aid donors encourage this research by committing in advance to help finance the purchase of suitable vaccines.

We argue that a key reason why pharmaceutical firms have been reluctant to invest in R&D on vaccines for diseases that primarily affect poor countries is that they fear they would not be able to sell the vaccine at prices that would cover their risk-adjusted costs. The low anticipated price reflects not only the poverty of the relevant populations, but also severe distortions in markets for vaccines for these diseases. Intellectual property rights for pharmaceuticals have historically been weak in low-income countries. Most vaccines sold in these countries are priced at pennies per dose, a tiny fraction of their social value—even measured in terms of what people with very low incomes would pay for the protection. Once pharmaceutical companies have invested in the research necessary to develop vaccines, governments often use their powers as regulators, dominant purchasers, and arbiters of intellectual property rights to keep prices low.

Research on vaccines is an "international public good" because the benefits of scientific and technological advances spill over to many nations. Hence, none of the many small countries that would benefit from a malaria, tuberculosis, or HIV vaccine has an incentive to encourage research by unilaterally offering to pay higher prices. And accordingly, private developers lack incentives to pursue socially valuable research on diseases primarily affecting low-income countries.

Incentive systems to encourage development of new products can be broadly classified as push programs, which subsidize research inputs, or pull programs, which reward developers for actually creating the desired product. Government-directed push programs are well suited for basic research. But for the later, applied stages of research, pull programs are also needed. With pull programs, money changes hands only after a successful product is developed. This approach of rewarding results gives researchers strong incentives to self-select projects that have the best chance of success. Pull programs also create incentives for researchers to focus on developing a vaccine, rather than pursuing ancillary goals, such as publishing journal articles. Moreover, appropriately designed pull programs can help ensure that, if new vaccines are developed, they will reach those people who need them. Several historical precedents, such as the Orphan Drug Act, suggest pull-like mechanisms can be effective tools for spurring product development.

The most attractive form of pull program is generally a commitment to fully or partially finance vaccine purchases for poor countries. Alternative pull approaches have significant disadvantages. Extending patents on other pharmaceuticals to reward developers of new products, for example, would place the entire burden of financing new products on the people who buy these other pharmaceuticals. Purchasing and distributing existing vaccines which are not being fully utilized would be a cost-effective way to save lives, but simply increasing prices for existing vaccines without explicit incentives for developing new ones would be an expensive and ineffective way to spur research on new vaccines.

For vaccine commitments to increase research activity, developers must believe that the sponsor will not renege once desired products have been developed and research costs sunk. If structured appropriately, these commitments can be legally binding contracts, as evidenced by legal precedents. The credibility of vaccine commitments can be further enhanced by specifying in advance the rules that govern the eligibility and pricing of vaccines, as well as by insulating the arbiters of these rules from political pressure.

Requiring candidate products to meet basic technical requirements, including approval by a competent national regulatory agency such as the U.S. Food and Drug Administration, would ensure that funds were spent only on effective vaccines. Requiring low-income countries to agree before a qualifying vaccine is used, and perhaps requiring them or other donors to contribute part of the production and distribution cost—would help ensure that products purchased by the program would be useful under actual field conditions.

One way to structure a vaccine commitment would be to guarantee a price of, say, $15–$20 per person for the first 200–250 million people immunized, in exchange for a commitment from the developer to subsequently drop the price in the poorest countries to a modest markup over manufacturing cost. A commitment of this size would offer firms an opportunity for sales comparable to those available in commercial markets. It would be extremely cost-effective, saving more lives than virtually any imaginable comparable health expenditure.

Vaccine commitments could be undertaken by international organizations such as the World Bank, by national governments, by private foundations such as the Bill & Melinda Gates Foundation, or by a combination of these groups. If a commitment to purchase vaccines failed to produce an effective vaccine, no donor funds would be spent; if it succeeded, tens of millions of lives would be saved at remarkably low cost.

This book lays out the rationale for a vaccine commitment and discusses how it could be designed. Chapter 2 reviews the disease environments in low-income countries and chapter 3 discusses the low level of research on diseases primarily affecting low income countries. (Readers familiar with health issues in developing countries may wish to skip these chapters.) In chapter 4 we discuss the market distortions that limit research in general and particularly limit research on vaccines against diseases that primarily affect poor countries. Chapters 5 and 6 outline the potential roles push and pull programs can play in addressing market failures in R&D. Chapter 7 reviews various types of pull programs and argues that commitments to help finance vaccine purchases would be most attractive. Chapters 8, 9, and 10 discuss how pull programs could be structured: how a candidate vaccine's eligibility for such a program could be determined, how much to pay for a vaccine, and how payments should be structured, for example to divide the reward between multiple providers. Chapter 11 explains how a similar approach might be used to induce R&D on other products, such as other medical technologies and technologies that could improve agricultural productivity in the tropics. Finally, chapter 12 discusses the political economy of a vaccine commitment and how it could be designed to meet the needs of possible sponsors.

■   ■   ■   ■

2. HEALTH IN LOW-INCOME COUNTRIES

We begin by outlining two sad characteristics of low-income country health environments: the prevalence of infectious diseases, and the weakness of health-care systems. We then discuss some of the leading infectious diseases in the developing world. Finally, we note that in spite of the obstacles, health has improved tremendously in low-income countries, due largely to the adoption of cheap, easy-to-use technologies such as vaccines.

The Disease Environment in Low-Income Countries

Poor countries face different disease environments than rich ones because of their geography, climate, limited resources, and often dysfunctional governments. A disproportionate share of low-income countries are in the tropics, and the high biodiversity of the environment gives rise to more numerous—and more virulent—infectious diseases, as well as to vectors like the African mosquitoes that spread malaria. Poverty leads to inadequate nutrition, sanitation, and education, all of which contribute to the spread of infectious diseases. Poor people often cannot afford to see a qualified doctor or to obtain drugs for infectious diseases that are easily cured in rich countries. Poor and often dysfunctional governments fail to provide clean water, sanitation, or public health programs such as mosquito control or effective antituberculosis campaigns.

As a result, infectious and parasitic diseases account for one-third of the disease burden in low-income countries—in fact, for over half of Africa's disease burden.[1] In contrast, infectious and parasitic diseases account for only 2.5 percent of the burden of disease in high-income countries (WHO 2003). The disease burden in high-income countries consists mainly of noncommunicable conditions disproportionately affecting the elderly, like cancer and cardiovascular disease, as seen in figure 1. Many other diseases are concentrated in low-income countries (table 1).[2] Middle-income countries (which include China as well as much of Latin America and Southeast Asia) have patterns of disease intermediate between these extremes.

WEAK HEALTH-CARE INFRASTRUCTURE

A key reason for the spread of infectious disease in low-income countries is weak health-care systems. Budgets are low and incentives for government health-care workers to do their jobs efficiently are weak. Private health delivery is clogged with quacks. These factors make it difficult to deliver all but simple forms of health care on a large scale.

Low-income sub-Saharan African nations spent only 6 percent of their average $300 per capita GDP on health—around $18 per person (World Bank 2001). In contrast, U.S. public and private health

---

[1] Burden of disease calculations measure the gap between current health status and an ideal in which all people live free of disease and disability into old age. The burden of different diseases can be compared across countries using the concept of Disability Adjusted Life Years (DALYs) (Murray and Lopez 1996a). DALYs serve as a quantitative measure of overall disease burden by combining years of potential life lost due to premature mortality and years of productive life lost due to disability. One DALY is equivalent to one year lost of healthy life.

[2] The high- and low-income classifications are as in the 2003 World Bank World Development Indicators, based on World Bank estimates of 2001 gross national income (GNI) per capita. Low-income implies a per capita GNI of less than $735 and includes almost all of South Asia and sub-Saharan Africa, while high-income implies a per capita GNI of $9,076 or more.

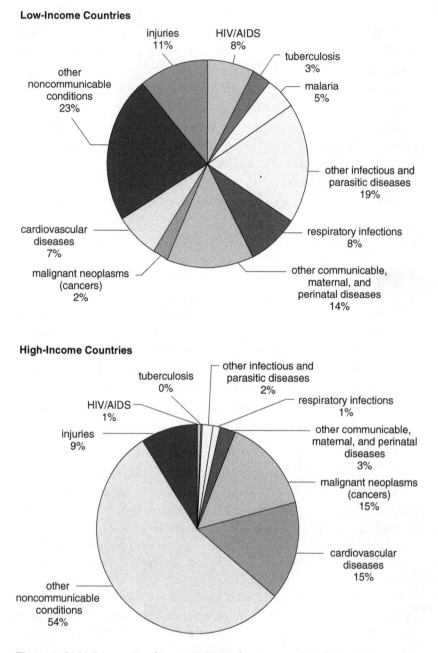

Figure 1. 2002 Disease Burdens (in DALYs) for Low- and High-Income Countries

TABLE 1

Diseases for Which at Least 99 Percent of the Global Burden Fell on Low- and
Middle-Income Countries in 1990

Disease	Deaths per Year	DALYs (thousands)
Diarrheal diseases[a]	2,124,032	62,227
Malaria	1,079,877	40,213
Measles	776,626	27,549
Pertussis	296,099	12,768
Tetanus	308,662	9,766
Syphilis	196,533	5,574
Lymphatic filariasis	404	5,549
Ancylostomiasis and necatoriasis (hookworm)	5,650	1,829
Leishmaniasis	40,913	1,810
Schistosomiasis	11,473	1,713
Trichuriasis	2,123	1,640
Trypanosomiasis	49,668	1,585
Trachoma	14	1,181
Onchocerciasis (river blindness)	—	951
Chagas disease	21,299	680
Dengue	12,037	433
Japanese encephalitis	3,502	426
Poliomyelitis	675	184
Leprosy	2,268	141
Diphtheria	3,394	114

Note: [a] Diarrheal diseases differ from the other diseases in this list because they are actually a variety of diseases, caused by different pathogens.

Source: Global Burden from WHO (1996a), cited in Lanjouw and Cockburn (2001), table 1.

spending constituted 13 percent of the country's almost $32,000 per capita income in 1998, for a total of more than $4,000 per person.

In many low-income countries, qualified medical personnel are scarce. Whereas the United States has 2.7 trained physicians per thousand people and Europe has 3.9, sub-Saharan Africa has only 0.1 (World Bank 2001).

Similarly, a large share of available health resources is often focused on a few high-quality facilities in the capital. While this means that the elite can receive high-quality care, it also means that the resources available to the bulk of the population, especially in rural areas, are considerably less than would be suggested even by the national averages just cited.

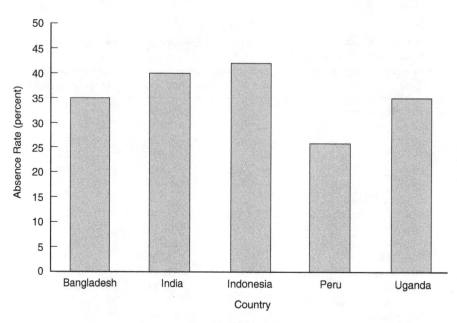

Figure 2. Absence Rate Among Health-Care Workers in Public Health Facilities (percent)

Note: Absence rate is percent of staff who are supposed to be present, but are not on the day of an unannounced visit.

Source: Chaudhury et al. (2004).

Government health-care systems are often dysfunctional. Medical personnel assigned to public clinics are often absent, particularly in rural areas. A study (Chaudhury et al. 2003) in which surprise visits were made to public primary health clinics in five low-income countries found that 25 to 40 percent of health workers were absent from their posts (see figure 2). Chaudhury et al. found that absence rates were particularly high among doctors, at over 40 percent on average. Moreover, clinics in low-income countries often lack drugs because salaries of health-care workers take priority in budget allocations and because drug procurement and distribution is inefficient or corrupt.

Many patients therefore rely on private health care, but private systems also function badly in the absence of basic quality regulation that is taken for granted in developed countries. Many private practitioners are untrained and prescribe inappropriate pharmaceuticals. A

1988 study by Kakar found three times more providers in the informal sector than in the formal sector in India. In a detailed study of medication in India, Phadke (1998) categorizes more than half of all drugs prescribed as "unnecessary" or "contraindicated." While self-prescription is not uncommon in the West, it is routine in the poorest countries, where rules requiring prescriptions are typically not enforced (Kamat and Nichter 1998). Many patients purchase and consume incomplete courses of medication, especially when symptoms subside after a partial course (Nichter and Nichter 1996). Drug overuse and misuse speed the development of drug-resistant forms of diseases because the most resistant microbes survive, and are then transmitted to others.

MALARIA, TUBERCULOSIS, AND HIV/AIDS

The combination of hospitable environment for infectious disease and the difficulties of appropriately delivering all but basic treatment through weak health-care systems leads to a terrible toll from infectious disease.

A host of diseases remain for the most part unknown to most people in high-income countries but continue to plague low-income countries, including Chagas' disease, leishmaniasis, trypanosomiasis (African sleeping sickness), onchocerciasis (African river blindness), and lymphatic filarsis. Chagas' disease, for example, which primarily plagues poor populations in rural areas of Latin America, was ranked by the World Bank in the 1990s as the most serious parasitic disease in Latin America, with a socioeconomic impact greater than that of all the other parasitic infections combined (for discussion, see Center for Global Development 2004).

Another prime example is schistosomiasis, a disease caused by intestinal worms that primarily afflicts rural populations in low-income countries which lack access to safe water and sanitation. The WHO estimates schistosomiasis affects 200 million people worldwide, 85 percent of them in Africa, and that 10 percent of the world's population (over half a billion people) are at risk of infection. In some areas the disease is so common that residents believe blood in one's urine (a signal of infection with one form of the disease) is a normal part of a child's development. The parasitic disease causes significant short-term illness, and, if left untreated, can severely impact health outcomes.

Historically, the control of schistosomiasis has been based on drug treatments, such as praziquantel. Treatment (given once a year) causes few side effects and costs less than a dollar per treatment. However, reinfection is rapid and drug treatment must be repeated every twelve months for people to remain clear of worms. Difficulties in delivery mean that millions go untreated. In recent years there have also been some reports of increasing tolerance and possible resistance to praziquantel (for example, Utzinger et al. 2000).

The three biggest killers, however, are malaria, tuberculosis, and HIV/AIDS, and we discuss each here.

Malaria

The World Health Organization (WHO) estimates that over 300 million people contract clinical malaria every year and 1.1 million die of the disease (WHO 2001).[3] Most of those killed are children. Although children who survive severe cases of malaria may suffer learning disorders and brain damage, those who manage to reach the age of five acquire some immunity. Those with this limited immunity rarely die from malaria, but they do become weak and lethargic with the disease in later life, making it hard for them to work. Pregnant women temporarily lose their acquired immunity and are at high risk from the disease.

Almost all malaria cases occur in low-income countries, and almost 90 percent of the victims live in sub-Saharan Africa (WHO 2000a). Africa carries most of the global burden of *falciparum*

---

[3] Other estimates are higher. WHO documents from the Rollback Malaria campaign cite 300–500 million cases of malaria and 1–2 million ensuing deaths annually. Breman and others (2001) argue that between 700,000 and 2.7 million people die of malaria each year, and that African children under five years of age living in malaria-endemic areas suffer between 400 million and 900 million incidents of acute febrile malaria each year.

malaria, the most lethal of the four strains, and is a breeding place for the mosquito that is the most effective transmitter of the disease.

Tuberculosis

Tuberculosis kills approximately 2 million people each year, 98 percent of them in low-income countries (WHO 2000b). An estimated one-third of the world's population is infected with latent tuberculosis, and 5 to 10 percent of them will show symptoms sometime in their lives (StopTB 2002). The disease spreads through droplets in the air, like the common cold. Active tuberculosis is usually a pulmonary infection, often leading to fatigue, weight loss, coughs producing blood and phlegm, fever, and night sweats. If not treated early, pulmonary tuberculosis can cause permanent lung damage and death.

Several drugs can be used to treat tuberculosis, but they must be taken regularly over six to eight months in order to be effective. Intermittent use leads to the development of drug-resistant strains of the bacillus. Those with drug-resistant tuberculosis require up to two years of treatment with very expensive medication, and most cases prove fatal. To combat the spread of drug-resistant tuberculosis, the WHO endorses a tuberculosis-control strategy called DOTS, or "directly observed treatment short-course," which is a six- to eight-month regimen of medication under the close supervision of a health worker or family member. The goal is to prevent inadequate or interrupted treatment, an all-too-common occurrence (Crofton et al. 2003).

Unfortunately, medical care for tuberculosis in poor countries is often terrible. Jishnu Das, a researcher at the World Bank, interviewed people in India with tuberculosis. One patient with spinal tuberculosis whom Das interviewed was not diagnosed until six months after her excruciating headaches and backaches began, and after previous doctors had treated her by dosing her with painkillers and by extracting teeth. Another tuberculosis patient whom Das interviewed was eight months pregnant when she was diagnosed. Family disagreement about whether to treat her in a public or a government facility delayed her therapy and she grew even sicker. Stigmatized by her illness, she believed neighbors' untutored claims that her breast milk would be infected. Her baby died of malnutrition shortly after birth.

Das found that people with multi-drug-resistant tuberculosis are often refused treatment at government clinics struggling to meet cure-rate standards. The drugs for multi-drug-resistant strains are funneled into the black market by doctors eager to supplement their salaries. Doctors can multiply their salaries fourfold by misdiagnosing a simple tuberculosis case as multi-drug-resistant, ordering the medication and selling it on the black market.

Compliance with DOTS regimens is often difficult to maintain, particularly if patients are experiencing side effects, which can include vomiting, jaundice, and confusion. In many cases, the symptoms of tuberculosis will go away after about a month of treatment, which leads some patients to believe they are cured. They stop taking the medication and relapse within a few weeks. In a randomized controlled trial conducted in Pakistan in 2001 (Walley et al. 2001), just under 500 adults with tuberculosis were randomly assigned to either direct observation of treatment by health workers through the country's National Tuberculosis Programme, direct observation of treatment by family members, or self-administered treatment. All three strategies led to similar outcomes (cure rates of 64 percent, 55 percent, and 62 percent, respectively) and treatment-completion rates (67 percent, 62 percent, and 65 percent, respectively). It is thus hardly surprising that multi-drug-resistant strains of tuberculosis are becoming increasingly common, especially in low-income countries. In 2000, cases of multi-drug-resistant tuberculosis had been reported in over one hundred different countries (Becerra et al. 2000). By the year 2003, some 400,000 of the 9 million reported cases of tuberculosis were multi-drug-resistant.

The spread of resistance poses a threat to high-income as well as to low-income countries. In the late 1980s and early 1990s, New York City saw a major epidemic of tuberculosis, with infection rates tripling and outbreaks of multi-drug-resistant tuberculosis occurring in many hospitals. New York City beat back the epidemic by spending over $1 billion to fight some 4,000 cases, and by rebuilding the tuberculosis treatment infrastructure that had been dismantled because of a belief that the disease had been effectively eradicated in North America (Sternberg 2003).

HIV/AIDS

The greatest toll of all is from HIV/AIDS. A recent *Washington Post* article (Wax 2003) reported the case of Lily Nanjala, age nine, and her brothers. Her HIV-positive mother, Beatrice, spent her last days teaching Lily how to do all the things she would need to survive on her own. The final lesson was how to dig her mother's grave.

Lily's case is notable for its cruelty, but similar cases are all too common. The lives of the Nanjala children reflect the experience of a generation of AIDS orphans. One in three residents of their area carry the HIV virus, and the young-adult generation has been devastated. The young and the old live among the graves, and orphans account for more than 10 percent of the population. Children struggle to work their land and to find food, often dropping out of school.

More than 42 million people are infected with HIV worldwide, over 95 percent of whom live in poor countries (UNAIDS 2002a). In 2002, about 3.1 million people died of AIDS. Approximately 5 million people were newly infected, with 70 percent of the new cases in sub-Saharan Africa (UNAIDS 2002a). HIV/AIDS is the leading cause of death in Africa, and the fourth largest cause of premature death globally. It has already orphaned over 13 million children, and this number is expected to double by 2010.

Figure 3 shows the estimated impact of HIV/AIDS on mortality in South Africa.

AIDS is disrupting entire societies, with potentially major consequences for long-run economic development. More than 30 percent of teachers are estimated to be HIV-positive in parts of Malawi and Uganda (Coombe 2000b). As AIDS continues to fell skilled workers in their prime, both public and private sector organizations must serially hire and train several workers for every position (Thurman 2001).

Worldwide, HIV is spread primarily through sexual contact. Transmission from mothers to children during labor and breast-feeding is

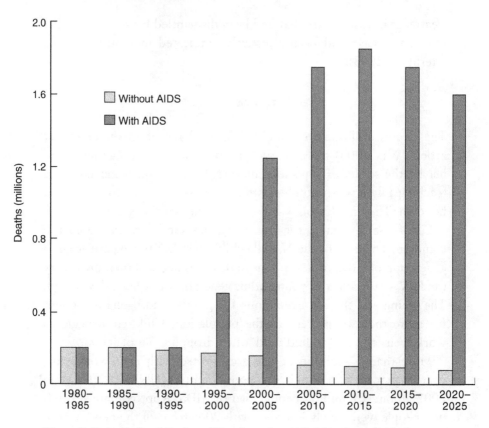

Figure 3. Estimated and Projected Deaths at Ages 15–34 in South Africa
Source: UNAIDS 2002b.

also common. UNICEF estimates that mother-to-child transmission of HIV through pregnancy, labor, delivery, and breast-feeding is responsible for over 90 percent of HIV infections in infants and children under the age of fifteen, and estimates that in 2001 there were 2.2 million pregnant women with HIV living in sub-Saharan Africa. In low-income countries, in the absence of any intervention to reduce the transmission of HIV from mother to child, 25 to 40 percent of women who are HIV-positive will transmit the virus to their children during delivery or after birth through breast-feeding (De Cock et al. 2000). In some countries, needle-sharing among intravenous drug users is also an important source of HIV transmission.

After a person is first infected with HIV, the virus multiplies rapidly in the body for a period of weeks or a few months until the immune system begins to block it, and the infection enters a latency period lasting anywhere from weeks to many years. Thereafter, the virus attacks immune system cells in large numbers, severely depressing the immune system and triggering the AIDS condition. Because their immune systems cannot protect them, people with AIDS are extremely vulnerable to cancer as well as to infectious diseases such as tuberculosis.

HIV exists in several different strains or genetic subtypes, called *clades*. Most infections in North America, Europe, Australia, and Latin America are clade B, while most infections in Africa are clade C.

Drugs are now available to prevent mother-to-child transmission and to treat HIV-infected people. Short-course treatment regimens of the drug Nevirapine have been found to reduce the risks of mother-to-child HIV transmission substantially, at a cost of only $4 per mother–infant pair (Marseilles et al. 1999). For example, a Ugandan study found that a single dose of Nevirapine given at the onset of labor, plus a single dose to the newborn within seventy-two hours of birth, reduced the risk of HIV transmission by half (Guay et al. 1999; Brooks et al. 2003). Yet services to prevent mother-to-child transmission of HIV remain virtually nonexistent in many heavily affected countries. Outside Botswana, less than 1 percent of pregnant women in sub-Saharan Africa receive information and treatment that would help them avoid transmitting HIV to their children (United Nations 2003). Worldwide, only an estimated 5 percent of the target population receives Nevirapine (Black et al. 2003).

In high-income countries, antiretroviral drugs (ARVs) are keeping a high proportion of HIV-infected people alive. The efficacy of ARVs depends in large part on adherence to the treatment regimen and to proper monitoring. The most favorable conditions for ARVs are structured programs with extensive counseling and physician care, as well as regular testing to monitor for disease progression and the onset of opportunistic infections. The toxicity of a given ARV can range from inconsequential to lethal. And the effects of such toxicity can complicate ARV therapy by leading the patient to associate the side effects with the treatment and thus discontinue use. Patients falling below 90–95 percent adherence to a therapeutic regime containing one of each of three classes of ARV drugs are at substantial risk of producing a resistant strain of HIV. While just one in five patients with adherence rates above 95 percent suffered virological failures within one year (Paterson et al. 2000), adherence to the recommended ARV regimen of less than 70 percent led four out of five patients to have virological rebounds.

In the event of a failed treatment course, a second line (and even a third line) of ARV therapy utilizing different drugs and potentially a different class of drugs can be implemented. But these drugs are typically very expensive.

Antiretrovirals are helping only a tiny proportion of people in low-income countries with HIV. As of this writing, approximately 50,000 people in Africa are currently taking ARV treatment. Yet an estimated 25 million people on the continent are infected with HIV, and 4.1 million have reached the stage of the disease in which the treatment would be medically appropriate (WHO 2003). The price of the drugs initially used to treat patients has come down dramatically, but delivering them and providing the necessary accompanying medical care and further treatment is the key administrative and financial challenge. The call by 133 Harvard faculty members for antiretroviral treatment estimated that purchasing and delivering antiretrovirals using a DOTS approach would cost $1,100 per person per year (Adams et al. 2001), while Connelly (2002) puts the figure for treating mine workers in South Africa at $1,800. Drug costs have come down since then and may fall even further. If we adjust the Harvard calculations for the most recently negotiated drug costs ($140 per year), the total cost per year falls to $613 (or $473 if drugs were provided at zero cost). Some argue that a less intensive treatment regime than the DOTS approach could be used as a way to further reduce costs, but this involves a trade-off, as less intensive treatment regimes would likely reduce the efficacy of the treatment for the individuals being treated and increase the probability of the emergence of HIV strains that are resistant to the antiretrovirals currently being used. Over and colleagues (2003) estimate the cost per patient-year in India would be about $500. These cost estimates should be put in the context of health budgets in low-income sub-Saharan African countries that average about $18 per person per year (World Bank 2001).

In middle-income countries such as South Africa, Botswana, and Brazil, ARVs may have a substantial impact. Yet most of the African countries with high HIV prevalence have much lower incomes—often only one-tenth as much. A number of pilot programs have achieved levels of adherence to ARV regimens in poor countries that are similar to those in developed countries. But these pilot programs typically enroll few patients and benefit from very intense levels of involvement from some of the best physicians and health workers in the country—and often from medical professionals from the developed world as well. It is unlikely that poor countries will successfully expand these programs to the majority of their populations using their own resources.

If rich countries spent even 1 percent of their income addressing health problems in low-income countries, they would be able to overcome many of the obstacles to effective delivery of antiretrovirals and save millions of lives. The track record, however, suggests that rich countries are unwilling to provide even the more modest sums necessary to save comparable numbers of lives using much cheaper, simpler technologies. The political salience of AIDS makes it easier to raise funds for AIDS than for other diseases, but based on current levels of funding it seems unlikely that the majority of people with AIDS in low-income African countries will benefit from antiretrovirals.

At a summit meeting held in Okinawa in 2000, the leaders of the G8 nations (United States, Japan, Britain, France, Italy, Germany, Canada, and Russia) pledged to achieve a series of goals by the year 2010, including a 25 percent reduction in HIV/AIDS among people aged twenty-five years or younger, a 50 percent reduction in prevalence and deaths from tuberculosis, and a 50 percent reduction in the burden of deaths associated with malaria. There is little prospect of meeting these targets using existing technologies alone. New drugs could help. But because resistance to drugs develops quickly and drug treatments are difficult to deliver in low-income countries, the best hope for deep, sustainable reductions in disease burden lies with the development of new vaccines. The next section discusses what can be achieved with this type of cheap, simple technology.

THE IMPACT OF CHEAP, SIMPLE TECHNOLOGIES

Despite severe problems, health in low-income countries has improved tremendously in recent decades, due in large part to the widespread adoption of cheap, easy-to-use technologies—with vaccination foremost among them. For example, in 1950 India's average life expectancies at birth were 39.4 for males and 38.0 for females; by 1998, the figures had jumped to 62.1 and 63.7, respectively (U.S. Census Bureau 2003). In 1950, 146 out of every 1,000 Indian children died before their first birthdays; by 2001 this figure had dropped to 67 per thousand (World Bank 2003). From 1960 to 2000, infant mortality rates per 1,000 births dropped from 107 to 10 in Chile, from 207 to 92 in The Gambia, from 126 to 58 in Ghana, and from 220 to 85 in Yemen (UNICEF 2003). In the past decade, Bangladesh has reduced infant mortality by one-half.

Today's low-income countries are much healthier than the industrialized countries were at comparable levels of development. For example, Vietnam has a life expectancy of sixty-nine years, despite a per capita income far below that of the United States in 1900—which at the time had a forty-seven-year life expectancy. Health can even improve despite economic decline.[4] For example, from 1972 to 1992, life expectancy in low-income sub-Saharan Africa increased by 10 percent (from 45 to 49 years), while infant mortality fell 30 percent from 133 per thousand to 93 per thousand (World Bank 2001). All this occurred despite a 13 percent fall in per capita GDP over the period as well as the beginning of the AIDS epidemic. The AIDS epidemic has since reversed the trend toward longer life expectancy in Africa. But in the rest of the developing world, health continues to improve.

---

[4] Data are from Balke and Gordon (1989), Johnston and Williamson (2002), Kurian (1994), and World Bank (2001). Even if GDP growth in the U.S. was underestimated by two percentage points annually, U.S. GDP in 1900 exceeded Vietnam's current GDP.

Poor countries have seen these health improvements largely thanks to the diffusion of new technologies. Analysis of worldwide health trends in the twentieth century suggests that most improvements resulted from technological advances rather than income growth. Preston (1975) estimates that income growth accounted for only 10 to 25 percent of the increase in life expectancy between the 1930s and 1960s, and suggests that technological advances were a key factor driving the improvement. Jamison et al. (2001) attribute only 5 percent of the decline in infant mortality rates from 1962 to 1987 to income growth and 21 percent to more education. They find that 74 percent was due to factors which reduced infant mortality holding constant income and education. The most important factor was likely the diffusion of technological advances in health, although other factors such as behavioral changes at a given level of income (e.g., a greater propensity to boil water) may also have played an important role.

Note that this stands in marked contrast to historical patterns of health improvement in the industrialized countries. There, health improved sharply before science began producing useful medicines. The process was largely driven by economic growth, improved incomes, and consequent improvements in nutrition, sanitation, and water supplies (Fogel 2002). The improvement in health in developing countries today is a quite different process, heavily dependent on the availability of cheap, simple, effective medical technologies.

Although a lack of consistent data makes it difficult to arrive at exact estimates of how many lives have been saved by these technologies, by all accounts their impact has been tremendous.[5]

Before the advent of antibiotics, in both developed and developing countries, millions of people died from diseases that are now easily treated. Antibiotics have virtually eliminated some diseases as major public health problems in high-income countries, and have dramatically cut their toll in low-income countries. For example, although pneumonia is still the number-one killer of children under five years

---

[5] Throughout this section we illustrate their impact using statistics compiled by the United Nation's Children Fund (UNICEF).

of age in poor countries, deaths from the disease have been in retreat since the introduction of inexpensive antibiotics. A one-week course of antibiotics used to treat pneumonia costs less than 25 cents. An estimated 40 percent of the target population currently receives antibiotic treatments for pneumonia (Black et al. 2003).

Contraceptives are another simple and inexpensive technology that has had a major impact on health in the developing world. UNICEF estimates 700 million women—two-thirds of the world's women of reproductive age who are married or in stable unions—are using some method of contraception. Contraceptive use by married women worldwide increased by nearly a fifth from 1990 to 2000; the percentage change in the developing world was roughly the same as for the world as a whole. Contraceptive use in sub-Saharan Africa jumped by nearly one-half—albeit from the very low starting point of 16 percent. The resulting fertility reductions have reduced maternal mortality. Moreover, since infant mortality is lower in small families, contraception has probably contributed to the reduction in infant mortality as well.

Diarrhea is a major killer of children in poor countries. Oral rehydration therapy (ORT) is a cheap and effective method of treating the dehydration caused by diarrhea. It consists of common salt and sugar mixed in clean water, which is given orally and serves to replace essential body fluids and salts. Although cause-specific mortality for diarrhea-related illnesses is difficult to measure, UNICEF (2004) estimates the use of oral rehydration therapy prevents one million child deaths annually. An estimated 20 percent of the target population (that is, people who would benefit from the therapy) is currently receiving ORT treatments (Black et al. 2003).

Simple and inexpensive supplements in populations suffering from vitamin A deficiency prevent blindness and decrease childhood deaths from illnesses such as diarrhea, measles, and acute respiratory infections by 23 percent. UNICEF estimates that between 1998 and 2000, over one million childhood deaths were avoided by the provision of vitamin A supplements. An estimated 55 percent of the target population currently receives vitamin A (Black et al. 2003).

Vaccines are perhaps the paradigmatic example of a simple technology requiring little training or expensive equipment to implement that has had a tremendous impact on health. Compared to drugs, vaccines are easier to deliver in low-income countries with weak health-care infrastructures. Vaccines do not require diagnosis for use, can be taken in a few doses instead of longer term regimens, and rarely have major side effects. Hence, they can be prescribed and distributed by health-care workers with limited training. Moreover, resistance rarely develops against vaccines.

The most dramatic success of vaccination was the defeat of smallpox in 1980. When the WHO began eradication efforts in 1967, the disease afflicted an estimated 15 million people annually—2 million of whom died. The WHO estimates that in the twenty years following eradication, the world was spared 350 million new infections and 40 million deaths.

A similar campaign is now underway for polio. According to WHO estimates, since the effort began in 1988, polio incidence has fallen from 350,000 cases in one hundred twenty-five countries to just 1,919 cases in seven countries (WHO 2004).

The main benefits of vaccination, however, come not from spectacular efforts to immunize enough people to eliminate infection, but through the far easier task of reaching enough people to hold down the toll from diseases that would otherwise be major killers. Seventy-four percent of the world's children now receive a standard package of cheap, off-patent vaccines through the World Health Organization's Expanded Program on Immunization (EPI).[6] These vaccines save some 3 million lives per year (Kim-Farley 1992)—almost 10,000 lives a day—and protect millions more from illness and permanent disability.[7] Although vaccination rates are uneven, UNICEF/WHO surveys report that 70 percent of infants in low-income countries received the three-dose DTP3 (diphtheria, tetanus, and pertussis) vaccine in 1995–99 (World Bank 2001). Vaccination rates are likely to improve over the near term because the Global Alliance for Vaccines

---

[6] Some believe 74 percent to be an overestimate.

[7] EPI vaccine preventable diseases include measles, poliomyelitis, neonatal tetanus, Haemophilus influenzae type b (Hib), rubella, and yellow fever.

and Immunization (GAVI), with major financing from the Bill & Melinda Gates Foundation, has begun a major effort to increase coverage of existing vaccines.

But no vaccines exist for malaria, schistosomiasis, or HIV. And although there is a vaccine for tuberculosis—BCG (Bacilleus of Calmette-Guérin)—it provides only short-term, imperfect protection against infection. There appears to be a geographic gradient in effectiveness—lower efficacy in warmer equatorial regions and higher in northern regions. Trials in Britain suggest effectiveness up to 80 percent, while trials in the southern United States and southern India suggest close to zero efficacy (WHO 1999d). A widely accepted explanation is that exposure to environmental mycobacteria, often found in warmer climates, reduces the protection provided by BCG.

■ ■ ■ ■

3. THE PAUCITY OF PRIVATE R&D TARGETED TO THE NEEDS OF LOW-INCOME COUNTRIES

Poor countries have benefited enormously from pharmaceuticals, and in particular from vaccines. However, most of these medicines have been developed in response to incentives provided by prospective sales in rich markets. The impact on low-income countries has been, for the most part, a fortunate byproduct. Little private R&D is targeted to solving health problems like malaria, tuberculosis, schistosomiasis, or Chagas' disease, which are concentrated in poor countries. Most of the research on HIV/AIDS is focused on drug treatments, rather than on vaccines that would almost certainly save many more lives in low-income countries. And when private firms conduct research on HIV vaccines, most is aimed at the strain of the virus common in richer countries.

Some have argued the reason for the paucity of research on vaccines for these diseases is that the scientific challenge they represent is insurmountable. While there is no doubt that the challenge is formidable, a number of recent scientific advances have increased the potential for developing vaccines against malaria, tuberculosis, and HIV.

THE EXTENT OF R&D TARGETED TO LOW-INCOME COUNTRIES

Of the 1,233 drugs licensed worldwide between 1975 and 1997, only 13 were for tropical diseases (Pecoul et al. 1999). Of these, five came from veterinary research, two were modifications of existing medicines, and two were produced for the U.S. military. Only four were developed by commercial pharmaceutical firms specifically for tropical diseases of humans. Half of all global health research and development in 1992 was undertaken by private industry—but less than .5 percent of that was spent on diseases specific to poor countries (WHO 1996).

Diseases such as schistosomiasis and malaria that primarily affect low-income countries are particularly starved of research funds. HIV/AIDS research, which is more active, has primarily been oriented toward antiretroviral treatments. While these have made a huge difference to people in developed economies, they are much more difficult and expensive to use than vaccines—and hence are reaching only a tiny minority of those living with HIV/AIDS in low-income countries.

To the extent that private vaccine research is conducted on HIV, it has been oriented mostly toward the HIV strains common in rich countries, rather than those common in Africa, where two-thirds of new infections occur.

The International AIDS Vaccine Initiative (IAVI) estimates total investment in AIDS vaccine R&D at $430–$470 million, but only $50–$70 million of this has come from private industry. The remainder is from governments and nongovernmental organizations. Total worldwide investment in malaria vaccine R&D remains an order of magnitude below that for an AIDS vaccine, at a total of only $60–$70 million combined from the public and private sectors (Moorthy et al. 2004). Smaller still are the R&D estimates for investment in a schistosomiasis vaccine: according to the WHO (2002c) only approximately $4.1 million in total R&D investments were made from 1997 to 2002 toward the development of a vaccine against schistosomiasis, and even that low level of investment was slowly declining each year.

Every year more than U.S. $70 billion is spent worldwide on health research and development by the public and private sectors, an estimated 10 percent of which is used for research into the health problems of 90 percent of the world's population (the so-called 10/90 gap) (Global Forum for Health Research 2002).

THE SCIENTIFIC POTENTIAL FOR NEW VACCINES

There is no doubt that the problems in developing effective vaccines against HIV/AIDS, tuberculosis, and malaria are formidable, in part because each has many variants and each evolves rapidly. Nonetheless, many scientists are optimistic about the long-run scientific prospects for vaccines. Recent advances in immunology, biochemistry, and biotechnology have provided new tools for understanding the immune response to these diseases, as well as for early testing of candidate vaccines in the lab and in animal models. Genetic sequencing of HIV and the organisms causing tuberculosis and malaria is complete.

Such advances may help scientists create vaccines that are more effective in the face of genetic diversity: for example, new vaccines may be able to target not just one but several different sites on disease organisms. This renewed interest in immunization, stemming in part from perceptions of increased technological opportunity, has led some to refer to the late twentieth century as a "golden age" for vaccines.

Candidate vaccines have been shown to protect against malaria in several rodent and primate models. Moreover, the human immune system can be primed against natural malaria infection, as demonstrated by the natural limited immunity against severe malaria that protects people who survive beyond childhood in malaria-epidemic areas. Since vaccines sensitize the immune system by mimicking natural infection, they may similarly provide protection against malaria.

A National Academy of Sciences report (1996) concluded that the development of a malaria vaccine is scientifically feasible. More recently, in a review article published in *The Lancet*, Moorthy et al. (2004) argue that, "although exact predictions are not possible, if sufficient funding were mobilized, a deployable, effective malaria vaccine is a realistic medium-term to long-term goal." Other scientists, however, are more pessimistic about the prospects for a malaria vaccine being developed through the research avenues currently being explored. As we will discuss later, instances in which there exists such a divergence of opinion on prospects for development are especially well-suited for pull programs such as vaccine commitments.

Candidate vaccines have been shown to induce protection against tuberculosis infection in animal models. The example of the BCG vaccine, which has been found to be effective against tuberculosis in Britain (though not in tropical climates), suggests that the human immune system can be primed against tuberculosis infection.

A number of candidate HIV vaccines have been shown to protect monkeys against infection and induce immune responses in humans. Indeed, two candidate vaccines reached the final (phase III) level of efficacy trials in 2003, although results were generally disappointing. Nonetheless, significant progress toward an HIV vaccine has been made (Nabel 2001). Dr. Anthony Fauci, Director of the U.S. National Institute of Allergy and Infectious Disease (NIAID), has noted that numerous promising HIV vaccine candidates exist (2003).

There may also be opportunities to develop vaccines against other diseases that disproportionately affect developing countries. Robert Bergquist (2004), former head of the Tropical Disease Research and Training division of the WHO, noted that most scientists in the field are convinced that it is possible to develop a vaccine against the parasite that causes schistosomiasis.

4. MARKET AND
GOVERNMENT FAILURES

In chapter 2 we argued that new vaccines against infectious diseases are desperately needed in poor countries, while in chapter 3 we discussed the dearth of investment in R&D for these vaccines. The technical difficulty of developing vaccines for malaria, tuberculosis, and HIV may have contributed to the reluctance to invest in the necessary research, but biotech and pharmaceutical firms take on many other difficult technical challenges given sufficient market incentives. As we have seen, few products are developed for diseases that primarily affect poor countries. In this chapter, we suggest that a key factor limiting research is the small size of markets. For vaccines against diseases that primarily affect poor countries, markets are small, not only because of the low incomes in these countries, but also due to severe market failures for vaccines and vaccine R&D. Public actions to correct these market failures, foreign assistance in particular, could be extremely cost-effective. Unfortunately, however, the market failures surrounding vaccines have been compounded by government failures.

As we will discuss, markets fail for vaccines and vaccine research for at least two reasons. First, vaccines are unlike most goods in that consumption by one person benefits many others by helping reduce the spread of disease. Second, the fruits of R&D are hard for developers to capture fully because they consist of intangible knowledge that others can copy. Patents can protect some of the benefits. But these benefits can only be realized by charging prices

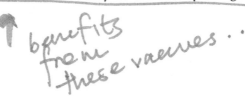

that far exceed manufacturing costs, which would mean that millions of people with low incomes would not obtain critical drugs and vaccines.

As a result, many poor countries have not chosen to create strong patent protection for pharmaceuticals, and this has made developers reluctant to develop products targeted to their markets. What is true in general for pharmaceuticals is particularly true for vaccines, which are nearly always purchased by governments or international agencies like UNICEF that use their power as dominant buyers to hold down prices.

These market and government failures indicate that the benefits to society of investments in vaccine R&D are many times greater than the benefits that accrue to the private investor. And this gap implies that assistance from governments or nonprofits that encourages vaccine research could potentially have a much higher payoff than other forms of aid to poor countries.

Markets in low-income countries are tiny. Africa now generates just 1 percent of pharmaceutical sales (see figure 4). Drug developers often do not even bother to take out patents in many small, poor countries (Attaran and Gillespie-White 2001). Connecticut alone spends more on health than the thirty-eight low-income nations of sub-Saharan Africa combined (author's calculations based on World Bank 2001; U.S. Census 2000).

WHY TARGET FOREIGN ASSISTANCE TO VACCINE R&D?

Economists often argue that, rather than targeting foreign aid toward the purchase of specific goods, it is better to let recipients choose how they spend the money. If we were thinking only about most tangible goods, this would make sense. If people placed a high value on consuming more protein, they might spend supplemental income on eggs. Farmers would then respond by raising more chickens and selling the eggs. On the other hand, if people really want shoes, factories would expand production to accommodate demand.

The key assumption driving the conclusion that providing money is

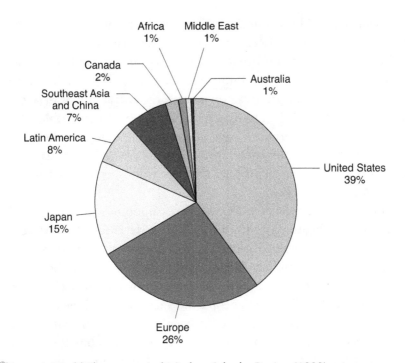

Figure 4. World Pharmaceutical Market, Sales by Region (1998)
Source: PhRMA *Industry Profile 2000* (adapted from figure 7-2)

better than providing goods in kind is that if people value a product more than it costs to produce, suppliers will serve the need. However, this is not likely to happen with new pharmaceuticals. Eggs or shoes differ from pharmaceuticals in two important ways. First, people who buy shoes gain all the benefits from their use, whereas the benefits of vaccination spill over to others because vaccines typically interfere with the spread of the disease.

Second, whereas the main expenses involved in producing shoes are raw materials, labor, and capital used in manufacturing, the main cost of producing new pharmaceuticals is R&D. The key output of biotech and pharmaceutical firms is not a physical product, but knowledge. And the use of knowledge is much harder to control than the use of tangible products like shoes. Once invented, pharmaceuticals can usually be manufactured relatively cheaply, so firms that have never invested in R&D may be the beneficiaries.[1]

These differences imply that providing money to people who put a high value on health would not generate the appropriate incentives for vaccine development. Economists call the total amount that individuals would be willing to pay for a product its "social" value. Private incentives to produce eggs correspond roughly to the social value of eggs—if consumers are willing to pay 15 cents each for more eggs, a farmer will produce the eggs as long as his costs are less than 15 cents.

This will not be the case for vaccines. Suppose one billion people were each willing to pay $40 to be free of malaria in light of the current risk of catching the disease. The social value of a malaria vaccine would then be $40 billion. But all those people would not be willing to pay $40 each for the vaccine because the value to unvaccinated individuals would fall as some people are vaccinated and the chance of being bitten by a mosquito that has been exposed to the parasite declined accordingly. Moreover, people may be able to buy the vaccine more cheaply from a "me-too" producer that free-rides off the research of the initial vaccine developer.

In the absence of any government role in the pharmaceutical industry, incentives for R&D would be insufficient due to the difficulties inherent in capturing the commercial fruits of knowledge. Suppose a pharmaceutical firm thought that if it spent $300 million it would have a 10 percent chance of developing a malaria vaccine that could be produced at negligible manufacturing cost. From society's point of view, a $300 million expenditure for a 10 percent chance of generating benefits valued at $40 billion would surely be worthwhile.

Nonetheless, the R&D might not be privately profitable. Suppose the vaccine could be copied and produced for 15 cents a dose. If the original developer tried to sell the vaccine at a price that would allow it to recoup its R&D costs, another company would grab its market.

---

[1] Making copycat versions of new vaccines is a greater technical challenge than making generic drugs, but it is still easier than doing the original research.

Understanding this, potential developers of the vaccine would be unlikely to make the investment in the first place.

Vaccines may also be under-consumed for other reasons. People seem much more willing to pay for treatment than prevention. Many potential consumers of vaccines in low-income countries are poorly educated, and, in any event, often have good reason to distrust governments claiming to serve their interests. Accordingly, they may place limited credence in official pronouncements about vaccination benefits. They may wait to take vaccines and observe what happens to neighbors who do. However, vaccination benefits, unlike drug treatment benefits, are not immediately visible, and many unvaccinated people will never contract the disease. Finally, the chief beneficiaries of vaccines are often children. And while most parents may appropriately take their children's welfare into account in making decisions, some do not.

THE PATENT TRADEOFF

Many countries have responded to the fact that R&D incentives would be inadequate in the absence of any government role in research by creating special property rights in knowledge—intellectual property rights (IPR) such as patents and copyrights. But these incentives come at a price. Patents make goods more expensive for consumers; specifically, they allow the owner of the patent to sell the product above the manufacturing cost without fear of being undercut by competitors. This implies that, at the margin, some goods will not be used even though their social value exceeds the cost of production.

It should not be surprising, then, that countries have made different decisions regarding the tradeoff between the benefits and costs of intellectual property protection. For example, during most of the nineteenth century, Switzerland had no patent system at all. In 1851 *The Economist* magazine ran an editorial asserting that "the public will learn that patents . . . cheat people by promising what they cannot perform. No possible good can ever come of a Patent Law, however admirably it may be framed" (reprinted in *The Economist* 2002). While the framers of the U.S. Constitution established provisions for patents, enforcement in the United States has varied. Eli Whitney, for example, had tremendous difficulty collecting royalties from farmers for the use of cotton gin technology that mechanically removed seeds from the raw fiber. Figure 5 depicts the circumstance of a vaccine patent holder who, in effect, is a monopolist because he alone has the right to sell the product.[2] The downward-sloping demand line shows consumers' willingness to pay for the vaccine. The lower horizontal line represents the cost of producing an additional dose of the vaccine, once the research costs have been incurred and the factory has been built. The patent holder attempting to maximize profit will choose the monopoly price that maximizes the size of A— the surplus of revenue over marginal manufacturing costs. Firms will invest in R&D for a vaccine if they believe A will exceed the risk-adjusted costs of vaccine research and development, along with the costs of building the factory.

That creates a dilemma. If society does not grant monopoly rights to the vaccine maker, the vaccine may never be developed and no one will be protected. On the other hand, if patent rights are in place, many people who would be willing to pay more than the cost of manufacturing an additional dose would not be able to afford the vaccine.

Note that if the vaccine maker could charge different prices to different consumers, it would have an incentive to serve those consumers who value the vaccine at more than the manufacturing cost but less than the monopoly price. In the extreme, if the manufacturer could charge each consumer exactly his or her willingness to pay for the product, it could obtain the entire revenue in the triangle in figure 5—and sell the vaccine to all who value it more than the marginal cost of manufacture.

This suggests that tiered pricing, in which sellers charge different prices to different classes of consumers, has many attractive features. And to a great extent, pharmaceutical manufacturers do charge lower prices in poor countries. But their ability to discriminate this way is limited by the fear that products sold at the lower price would be reimported by consumers in rich countries.

---

[2] This analysis abstracts from the spillover benefits of vaccination.

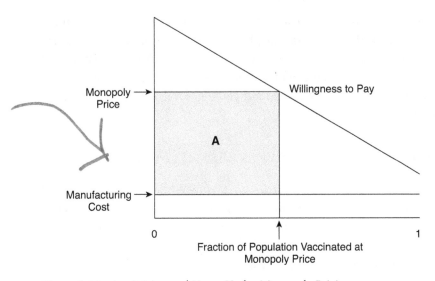

Figure 5. Vaccine Pricing and Usage Under Monopoly Pricing

More important, drug makers' willingness to price discriminate in this way is tempered by the fear of political backlash in richer countries. It is difficult for pharmaceutical companies to justify charging much higher prices in one country than in another. For example, after Senator Paula Hawkins of Florida asked a major vaccine manufacturer how it could justify charging nearly three times as much to the U.S. government for vaccines as to foreign countries, U.S. manufacturers stopped submitting bids to UNICEF to supply vaccines (Mitchell, Philipose, and Sanford 1993; U.S. Congress, Senate 1982). When President Clinton announced his plan to immunize all children against a standard list of diseases in 1993, he said, "I cannot believe that anyone seriously believes that America should manufacture vaccines for the world, *sell them cheaper in foreign countries*, and immunize fewer kids as a percentage of the population than any nation in this hemisphere but Bolivia and Haiti" (Mitchell et al. 1993; italics added).

In the face of such statements, the reluctance of pharmaceutical companies to discount prices in poor countries is unsurprising. And recently there has been a strong movement in the United States to allow imports of drugs from Canada, which may further discourage pharmaceutical firms from sharply differentiating prices across countries. In any case, though useful for diseases that affect industrialized countries, tiered pricing would not encourage research on diseases such as malaria, tuberculosis, and clade C HIV, which primarily affect poor countries.

LOW-INCOME COUNTRIES AND INTELLECTUAL PROPERTY

Most large low-income countries have allowed firms to copy and sell pharmaceuticals, thus keeping pharmaceutical prices low by withholding effective patent protection (Siebeck et al. 1990). For example, under India's Patents Act of 1970, pharmaceutical products cannot (as of writing) be patented. India thus allows pharmaceuticals patented elsewhere to be freely copied and marketed there (Lanjouw 1996).[3] The late Indian Prime Minister Indira Gandhi announced in 1975, "My idea of a better-ordered world is one in which medical discoveries would be free of patents and there will be no profiteering from life and death" (Bailey 2001).

The 1994 Agreement on Trade-Related Aspects of Intellectual Property Rights (TRIPS), Annex 1C to the agreement establishing the World Trade Organization (WTO), required all member-countries to provide twenty-year patent protection for pharmaceuticals (WTO 2001a). The TRIPS agreement was championed by the United States, but other countries fought to include provisions to limit TRIPS. Indeed, Article 31 of the original 1994 TRIPS Agreement states that the patent requirement "may be waived by a Member in the case of a national emergency or other circumstances of extreme urgency or in cases of public non-commercial use."

The issue came to a head when South Africa and Brazil fought for the right to impose compulsory licensing on AIDS drugs. AIDS activists in rich countries backed this claim. As a result of public outcry, the United States dropped its dispute with South Africa over the

---

[3] Patents on techniques for manufacturing pharmaceuticals were allowed, but this still meant that Indian firms could reverse engineer pharmaceuticals patented by others.

country's imports of pharmaceutical products from countries with weaker patent laws and abandoned its dispute with Brazil over unlicensed manufacture of drugs still under patent. Pharmaceutical firms, faced with a public relations nightmare, eventually cut prices in least-developed countries to zero- or negative-profit levels.

The backlash over pricing of AIDS drugs eventually led WTO negotiators to adopt a separate declaration on TRIPS and public health. This declaration extended the transition period for instituting patent protection for pharmaceuticals to 2016 in the poorest countries (WTO 2001b). And enforcement of even that deadline could be delayed. In August 2003, WTO governments agreed to allow any member to export pharmaceutical products made under compulsory licenses within the terms set out in the WTO decision. In any event, enforcement of TRIPS provisions relies on countries bringing suits, and it is far from clear that countries will bring such suits.

Whatever the overall benefits of decisions regarding compulsory licensing of AIDS drugs, there is little doubt that pharmaceutical developers will see the weakening of patent protection as a precedent that could be used to obtain vaccines and other drugs at low prices. Under the circumstances, pharmaceutical companies may be reluctant to invest heavily in drug or vaccine research for diseases that primarily affect poor countries.

In our view, the debate over drug pricing and intellectual property rights in low-income countries has shed more heat than light. The debate pits the goal of creating R&D incentives to develop new pharmaceuticals against the goal of ensuring wide access to pharmaceuticals once they are developed. Both goals are critical, and the world needs new institutions that will promote both. In the second half of this book, we discuss how commitments to purchase needed vaccines could advance both goals simultaneously.

Even if patents were enforced, research incentives would still be suboptimal—particularly for vaccines. Once a pharmaceutical company invests millions in risky efforts to develop a new drug or vaccine, other companies often create competing products by altering the original approach just enough to avoid patent infringement. Such "me-too" compounds drive down the price of (and thus the return to) the original.

In many industries, such as computer software, the first company to fill a niche gains a customer base. And the resulting "first-mover" advantages can, in part, compensate for competitors' end runs around its intellectual property rights. However, first-mover advantages are limited in the case of vaccines because they are usually purchased by governments and international organizations not known for their brand loyalty. Moreover, there are very few buyers of vaccines. The resulting market power on the buyers' side offsets the value of patent protection—and thus, the incentives to innovate.

Finally, as Kremer and Snyder (2003) show, firms may be reluctant to invest in vaccines relative to drugs because, if individuals differ in their risk of contracting a disease, firms will not be fully rewarded for the benefits of vaccines. To see why, consider a simple example. Suppose that out of 100 million people, 90 million have a 10 percent chance of contracting a disease and 10 million have a 100 percent chance. Suppose, too, that individuals are willing to pay $10 to reduce their chances of getting the disease by 10 percent and $100 to be cured of the disease if they contract it.

A firm selling a drug cure would be able to sell to all people who contract the disease at a price of $100. Some 19 million consumers will get the disease (all 10 million of the high-risk consumers, along with 9 million low-risk consumers). So total revenue will be $1.9 billion. In this hypothetical example, this corresponds to the social value of the product.

In contrast, a firm developing a vaccine could either charge $100 and sell it only to the 10 million high-risk consumers, or charge $10 and sell to all 100 million consumers. Either way, the firm's revenue would be $1 billion, or only about half the social value of the product. Calibrations reported by Kremer and Snyder (2003) suggest that this factor alone could cause revenue from drugs against sexually transmitted diseases to exceed that from vaccines by a factor of four.

The problems outlined above, in particular (a) being unable to capture the "externalities" from vaccine consumption and (b) finding it difficult to enforce property rights associated with knowledge, mean that the return to private vaccine developers is much less than the social value of vaccines. This, in turn, means developers will pursue far

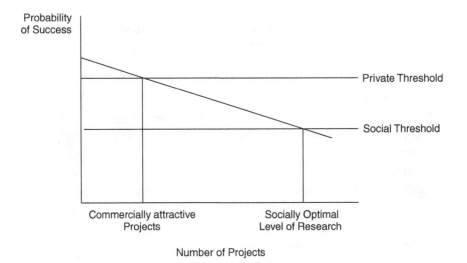

Figure 6. Commercially Attractive Research Projects and Socially Worthwhile Projects

fewer research opportunities than would be socially optimal. Companies will invest in R&D on a project if the probability of success, times the expected private return to a successful vaccine, exceeds the R&D costs. However, it is worthwhile for society for the project to be undertaken if the probability of success, times the *social* value of the vaccine (if it is successful), is greater than the R&D costs.

Since the private returns are so much less than the social returns, many projects that would be worthwhile for society are not commercially attractive for private developers (see figure 6). As figure 6 illustrates, commercially attractive projects are those with relatively high probability of success where R&D costs can (on average) be recouped given the private returns from the vaccine. However, if the social returns are higher than private returns, the threshold at which it is worthwhile to pursue a research project is correspondingly lower. Thus, the number of projects that should be pursued is higher than the number that will be pursued in the absence of some kind of intervention. In other words, it may be in society's interest to invest in vaccine projects that have much lower probabilities of success than would be needed to motivate private investors.

SOCIAL VERSUS PRIVATE RETURN:
SOME QUANTITATIVE ESTIMATES

How large is the gap between the private return and the social return to vaccine innovation? Economists have estimated that, even with intellectual property rights in place, social returns on R&D are typically twice the returns realized by private developers (Nadiri 1993; Mansfield et al. 1977). But the market failures for vaccines are much greater than for typical products. For purposes of illustration, consider a hypothetical one-dose malaria vaccine that is 100 percent effective and provides immunity for twenty years, as modeled by an extension to Glennerster and Kremer (2001).

The cost-effectiveness of a health intervention is often assessed in terms of the cost per Disability Adjusted Life Year (DALY) saved. Health interventions in the United States are often considered cost effective at $50,000 to $100,000 per DALY (Neumann et al. 2000). In its 1993 World Development Report, the World Bank implicitly treated health interventions as highly cost-effective for poor countries if they cost less than $100 per DALY saved. Others have suggested using a cutoff equal to a country's per capita GNP (WHO Regional Office for South-East Asia 2002), and several have noted the World Bank may use this as a rule of thumb (GAVI 2004; WHO 2000d).

The World Health Organization (WHO) recently estimated that malaria imposes a burden of 45 million DALYs per year (WHO 2000a). A vaccine would be ideally targeted to children under five, who have not yet developed limited natural immunity, and women pregnant with their first child, whose immune systems are suppressed. Annually, some 86 million children are born and 21 million women become pregnant for the first time in low- and middle-income countries with sufficiently high prevalence of malaria to make vaccination cost-effective under a wide range of assumptions. Assuming that after a transition period newborns receive the vaccine at a rate comparable to that of the third dose of the diphtheria, tetanus, and pertussis (DTP3) vaccine, a standard benchmark measure of immunization coverage, and that first-time mothers receive the vaccine at a rate comparable to the tetanus toxoid (TT2) vaccine, 75 million people would eventually be immunized annually, saving over 30 million DALYs per year.

If we make the assumption that alternative health expenditures could save a DALY for as little as $100, immunizing these 75 million people against malaria would be attractive relative to other health expenditures even if the vaccine were priced as high as $40 per vaccinated person. This would translate into revenues of $3 billion annually in perpetuity. And these figures do not account for the societal benefits of reduced disease transmission, or the potential economic benefits of reducing malaria prevalence beyond impact on individuals suffering from the disease.

Sales of childhood vaccines have historically totaled only $200 million annually in low-income countries (World Bank AIDS Vaccine Task Force 2000)—a tiny fraction of the $3 billion estimate of what a malaria vaccine alone would be worth to society at even $100 per DALY.

A vaccine under patent would likely generate greater revenues than the off-patent vaccines currently included in the WHO's Expanded Programme on Immunizations (EPI), which have historically sold for about 50 cents per dose (Robbins and Freeman 1988). But there are plainly limits to how much a vaccine developer could expect to receive under the current system: when the hepatitis B vaccine was introduced at $30 per dose, it was rarely used in low-income countries (Muraskin 1995; Galambos 1995). Even at a dollar or two per dose, hepatitis B and *Haemophilus influenzae* b vaccines did not reach most children in the poorest countries (General Accounting Office 1999). In fact, given current vaccine prices and health budgets in poor countries, a malaria vaccine developer would likely earn revenues less than one-tenth or one-twentieth of the $40 per immunized person cost-effectiveness threshold.

From the standpoint of society as a whole, it would be cost-effective to develop a malaria vaccine even if the necessary R&D were risky and expensive enough to require a price of $40 per immunized person—a total market of $3 billion annually, in perpetuity—to recoup the costs. But vaccines are likely to be commercially attractive investments only if developers expect risk-adjusted costs—including

R&D costs—to be less than the $2 or so per dose that private developers might earn.

The Role of Public Purchases

Large-scale government purchases could, in theory, compensate for the private market failures that reduce both R&D incentives and use of vaccines already developed. But to address the market failures, governments would need to pay high prices to vaccine producers (often unpopular multinationals) and to subsidize delivery to consumers. Simply establishing intellectual property rights for vaccines and allowing private sales would lead to underconsumption of vaccines, while simply buying vaccines as cheaply as possible and subsidizing consumption would undermine R&D incentives.

Because vaccine development is expensive while manufacturing additional vaccine doses at the margin is cheap, large government purchases at prices above manufacturing costs (but below monopoly prices) could make both vaccine producers and consumers better off than they would be in a market that allowed producers to sell at monopoly prices. If the government bought enough vaccine, manufacturers might be better off than with monopoly pricing. So government purchases could actually increase R&D incentives, even if the government paid less than the monopoly price.

To see why large public purchases that expand the market and bring down the cost per person could make everyone better off, suppose that willingness to pay is proportional to income and that the government agrees to pay the vaccine manufacturer an amount equal to the sum of areas A, B, C, and D (figure 7) in exchange for enough vaccine for the entire population. If these purchases are funded by an income tax, with all people who would have paid the monopoly price paying just under that price and all others paying just over the actual production cost, both vaccine producers and the general public would be better off. The sum of areas D and E is the social benefit of the vaccine purchase program.

This hypothetical government is not bargaining for the lowest possible price, but for a price that makes both producers and consumers better off. However, actual governments typically pay much less for

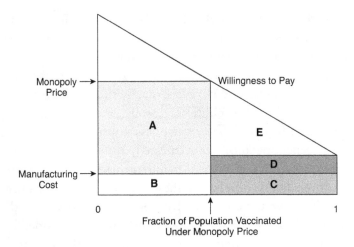

Figure 7. Public Purchases of Vaccines

two reasons. First, even if a government places a high value on having a vaccine, after developers have sunk their R&D investments, governments have every incentive to force prices down to a level that covers only manufacturing costs—and not the R&D expenses. This is known as the time-consistency problem in economics. Moreover, governments are typically in a position to drive very hard bargains because they often serve as primary purchasers of vaccines, as well as regulating pharmaceuticals and enforcing intellectual property rights. This helps explain why the value of all sales of childhood vaccines in low-income countries has historically been only $200 million annually (World Bank AIDS Vaccine Task Force 2000).

Second, because vaccine R&D is a global public good, each country has an incentive to "free-ride" from research financed by other countries' governments or induced by other countries' greater commitment to protect intellectual property. Each country benefits from a new vaccine, but each prefers that others pay the costs of development. The dearth of vaccine research for malaria, tuberculosis, and African HIV clades thus stems not only from the abject poverty of the afflicted countries, but from free-rider problems that plague the production of all "public" goods.

Large countries, like the United States, know they risk inhibiting research if they free-ride. But small countries, like Uganda, know their individual actions barely affect total research incentives. And yet pharmaceutical companies have little incentive to develop malaria vaccines if every African country flouts patents.

Aside from these time-consistency and global public good problems, some governments do not place much priority on obtaining and distributing vaccines for political reasons. Because vaccines yield widely diffused benefits, they receive less political support than expenditures benefiting more concentrated, better organized groups. For example, building a hospital mainly provides highly valued services to those living nearby, so these residents may organize and lobby for its construction. Similarly, people infected with a disease like AIDS will lobby for subsidized treatment. Or consider healthcare workers, who are often organized in unions. When health budgets are cut, they usually mobilize to protect salaries and jobs of existing workers.

The world needs new institutions that both encourage new pharmaceutical development and provide the poor with access to these new pharmaceuticals. To get from here to there, we must find ways to align the interests of pharmaceutical companies for a return on any investment with the interest of the public in rapid innovation and wide distribution of the products.

Such enabling institutions would ideally address both time-consistency and free-riding problems. The time-consistency problem suggests that the world cannot wait until a vaccine is nearly ready to address incentive issues. The free-riding problem suggests that if individual countries act in their narrow self-interest, they will slow innovation. Accordingly, solutions will have to come from entities with broader mandates—be they international organizations, bilateral aid programs, or private foundations.

5. THE ROLE OF
PUSH PROGRAMS

The literature on research incentives distinguishes between *push* and *pull* approaches. *Push programs* subsidize research inputs through means such as grants to academics, public equity investments in product development, tax credits for R&D investment, and outlays for government laboratories. *Pull programs* increase the rewards for developing specific products by committing to reward success—for example, by guaranteeing to purchase a certain quantity and/or agreeing to pay at least a minimum price for the product. The distinction, then, is roughly between paying for research inputs and paying for research outputs.

The R&D system in high-income countries, which has been very successful in generating innovation, involves a combination of push and pull. Government organizations such as the U.S. National Institutes for Health (NIH) support basic research, and the private sector is stimulated to turn these into usable products by the promise of the market protected by patents. Pharmaceutical firms' primary incentive for investing in R&D is the prospect of future sales. Applying the same principle to vaccines and drugs for poor countries would suggest using push programs for basic research and pull programs to encourage biotech and pharmaceutical firms to turn this research into vaccines and drugs. A number of push programs currently support research on diseases of the poor, including the International AIDS Vaccine Initiative (IAVI), the Medicines for Malaria Venture (MMV), and the Malaria Vaccine Initiative (MVI).

In contrast, there are no programs in place currently to provide credible assurances to potential developers of effective malaria, tuberculosis, or HIV vaccines that they will be appropriately rewarded.

In this chapter, we review two examples of push programs—one successful, and one unsuccessful, and use these to illustrate incentive issues under push programs. The next chapter discusses the role of pull programs.

MENINGOCOCCAL MENINGITIS: AN EXAMPLE OF A SUCCESSFUL PUSH PROGRAM

Meningococcal meningitis kills roughly 10 percent of those who become ill, even with aggressive treatment. In poor countries the mortality range runs 20–40 percent. Among victims who survive, one in four develops cerebral palsy, speech defects, or other forms of permanent brain damage. Shortly after America's entry into World War II, type A meningococcal bacteria caused a severe epidemic in the United States.

Elvin Kabat and Michael Heidelberger discovered the immunizing capabilities of pneumococcal polysaccharides, but this vaccine proved too weak to stimulate antibody response in the immune system. Also, antibiotics were discovered that were effective in treating meningococcal infections. Consequently, in the 1940s scientists aborted efforts to make a meningococcal vaccine. However, in the early 1960s, the emergence of meningococcal strains resistant to the antibiotics, along with increased incidence of the disease among the military (25.2 per 100,000 persons per year), led scientists at the Walter Reed Army Institute (WRAIR) to develop a meningococcal vaccine.

In 1969, three physicians at WRAIR, Malcom Artenstein, Irving Goldschneider, and Emil Gotschlich, extended the basic research of Kabat and Heidelberger to develop a polysaccharide vaccine against meningococcal type A and type C disease. The vaccine drastically lowered the incidence of infections among U.S. Army personnel, and by 1971, meningococcal polysaccharide vaccination was required for all recruits. Today, rates of meningococcal disease remain low in the military—0.51 per 100,000 persons per year. Approximately 180,000 inductees receive a single dose of meningococcal polysaccharide vaccine each year.

While the vaccine provides imperfect protection and is not recommended for the general population, it is given to those at high risk—for example, travelers to West Africa and people with immune disorders. In addition, the Advisory Committee on Immunization Practices (ACIP) recommended in 1999 that health-care providers at universities make vaccination against meningitis readily available to students. The counsel followed studies showing that college freshmen were at relatively high risk of contracting the disease. Since 1997, many colleges have required meningococcal polysaccharide vaccination for freshmen—and, in particular, for those who live in dormitories.

Other examples of successful push programs include research funded by the Consultative Group on International Agricultural Research (CGIAR), which led to the development of green revolution seeds. However, push programs also face a number of serious practical problems.

A Cautionary Tale: The USAID Malaria Vaccine Program

In the 1980s, the U.S. Agency for International Development (USAID) put considerable effort and millions of dollars into developing a malaria vaccine. Instead of a vaccine, the program yielded a dramatic illustration of the potential problems with push programs (Desowitz 1991).

USAID initially funded one research team that developed a candidate vaccine. Their tests found that only two of nine volunteers were protected from malaria; moreover, the results suggested that the vaccine would generate serious side effects. Yet these results led USAID to claim a "major breakthrough in the development of a vaccine against the most deadly form of malaria in human beings." The agency asserted that "the vaccine should be ready for use around the world, especially in developing countries, within five years" (Desowitz 1991).

That was in 1984. Today, the world is still waiting for a malaria vaccine.

Early work by a second team yielded disappointing results. Nonetheless, the principal investigator argued that his approach was still worth pursuing and requested an additional $2.38 million from USAID. The outside experts assigned to review the project recommended that the research not be funded. Nonetheless, USAID's malaria vaccine project director told the USAID Office of Procurement that the experts "had endorsed the scientific methodology and the exceptional qualifications and experience of the researchers" (Desowitz 1991). Once the grant came through, the principal investigator transferred grant funds to his personal account. He was later indicted for theft.

The independent evaluations of a third proposal characterized it as both mediocre and unrealistic. The USAID project director ignored these conclusions and arranged for the project to be fully funded. The principal investigator and his administrative assistant were later indicted for theft and criminal conspiracy in diverting money from the grant to their personal accounts. Two months before his arrest, the Rockefeller Foundation had provided the principal investigator with a $750,000 research grant. And on the very day of his arrest, USAID announced it was giving him an additional $1.65 million for research.

By 1986, USAID had spent more than $60 million on its malaria vaccine efforts, with little to show for it. But that is not the end of this doleful story. Since USAID believed that many suitable candidate malaria vaccines would soon be ready for testing, the agency began logistical preparations for vaccine trials, including the process of obtaining monkeys to serve as test subjects. USAID's malaria vaccine project director, James Erickson, received a kickback for arranging one such contract with an associate. Erickson eventually pleaded guilty to accepting an illegal gratuity, filing false tax returns, and making false statements (Brown 1990).

USAID had also arranged for the American Institute of Biological Science (AIBS) to provide oversight. This proved ineffective, not least because Erickson and the AIBS-assigned project manager were having an affair (Anderson 1989).

The biggest potential tragedy is that the USAID malaria scandal could have affected future allocations of funding on tropical disease research, leading good projects to be thrown out with bad ones. In 1994, the Clinton administration announced a 40 percent cut in funding for research on tropical diseases (Hilts 1994).

INCENTIVES UNDER PUSH PROGRAMS

While the USAID malaria case is extreme, it illustrates a number of general problems with push programs that prevent them from fully realizing the potentially enormous social return to research. Because push programs pay for research inputs rather than results, decisions must be made about where to commit funds before a product is actually developed. These decisions are in the hands of administrators who must rely on information from those with vested interests in the decisions.

Researchers funded on the basis of an outsiders' assessment of potential rather than for actual product delivery have incentives to exaggerate the prospects that their approach will succeed, and once they are funded, may sometimes even have incentives to divert resources away from the search for the desired product. Similar incentive problems occur regardless of whether aid comes in the form of grants, or targeted R&D tax credits for research, or government capital investments in private research programs in exchange for a share of profits or a commitment to price the output below market rates. Each of these policy interventions has its associated problems, which are discussed next. Nevertheless, it is important to bear in mind that, given the very large gap between private and social returns to research on vaccines, push programs typically have strong positive returns even if they cannot realize the full potential return that would be theoretically possible in the absence of the inefficiencies detailed in this discussion.

Publicly Funded Research

Even after it was clear that USAID's malaria vaccine initiative was not going well, researchers kept requesting added funding and administrators kept approving it. This is partly because researchers have a natural tendency to look favorably on the promise of their own work and because administrators have incentives to preserve and expand their programs.

Even if research administrators manage to choose wisely among scientific approaches at the outset, they may develop a bureaucratic stake in their judgments and fail to revise them in light of subsequent evidence. If results from a research project that initially appears promising turn out to be disappointing, a private firm has bottom-line incentives to shut the project down. A public program is more likely to acquire its own bureaucratic momentum, which can lead governments to throw good money after bad.

The problem of selecting research projects exists not only on the level of deciding which research avenues are most promising, but deciding which diseases and products will be targeted. Under a system of grant-financed research, advocates for particular diseases and scientists working on these diseases have an interest in portraying research opportunities favorably. Elected officials and the public are thus likely to find it very difficult to assess the scientific opportunities for research on malaria, tuberculosis, and HIV/AIDS vaccines and drugs. And decision-makers may wind up financing ideas with only a small prospect of success—or worse, failing to fund promising research because they do not have confidence in the objectivity of its backers. By contrast, a pull system rewards developers only if they generate the desired product. Thus, firms considering research investments have a strong incentive to assess the prospects for success in realistic terms.

Although criminal activity in this context is unusual, the other problem with USAID's malaria push program was that researchers misappropriated funds. But a lesser parallel problem is common with aid tied to research grants: researchers often have incentives to stray from the task, devoting effort to preparing the next grant application or to work on unrelated projects that will advance their careers.

Finally, when governments allocate research funds up front, they may be inclined to base decisions on political, rather than scientific, considerations. For example, there may be pressure to spend funds in specific states or congressional districts. The analogue for internationally supported research on malaria, tuberculosis, and HIV/AIDS is political pressure to allocate research expenditures to specific countries. With pull programs, by contrast, the sponsors promise to pay for a viable vaccine no matter who develops it or where.

The problems with publicly funded push programs plainly extend beyond the USAID malaria vaccine program to government efforts to pick winners in commercial R&D. The record of projects that have received intensive public investment is littered with failures ranging from supersonic transport to the nuclear breeder reactor to the 1970s oil shale program, although there are some notable successes such as the communications satellites technology which emerged during the 1960s (see Cohen and Noll 1981). Surveys suggest that while both government and private R&D have strong positive returns on average, the rate of return on private R&D is much greater (Nadiri 1993; Nadiri and Mamuneas 1994; Bernstein and Nadiri 1988, 1991).

Government Equity Investments in Private Research

One variant on direct government research financing is investing government funds in private firms that conduct desired research. The intent is to inject market discipline into the research process, thus overcoming some of the incentive problems associated with direct government financing. However, public sector equity investments in product development encounter the same fundamental problems as research funded by grants. Indeed, firms' incentives to misrepresent their chances for success are in some ways exacerbated. Companies that believe they have identified profitable projects will be least inclined to seek public sector investments, which would dilute the principals' equity stake. On the other hand, companies that are least confident will be most inclined to hedge the risk with government equity funds. As with direct government support, there is a danger that public equity investment will be subject to political influence.

Targeted R&D Tax Credits

Some have proposed targeting R&D tax credits toward research for drugs and vaccines for malaria, tuberculosis, and HIV. For example, in the United States the proposed Vaccines for the New Millennium

Act of 2001 included a 30 percent tax credit on company R&D expenditures for vaccines for HIV, tuberculosis, and malaria. Such credits would likely boost R&D expenditures, at least at the margin. However, because these tax credits would reward research inputs and not results, they would be subject to many of the problems of other push programs.

First, R&D tax credits do not improve access to products once they are developed. Patent rights for a malaria or HIV vaccine developed by a company that received the credit would remain with the company for the usual period of market exclusivity. And if intellectual property rights were respected, the price of the vaccine might well be high enough to deny the vast majority of residents of poor countries the benefit from the vaccine during the life of the patent.

Second, R&D tax credits may not create incentives to develop products appropriate for low-income countries because markets in rich countries are more likely to be profitable. Most new HIV infections occur in Africa, where clade C dominates. However, commercial vaccine development is focused on clade B, which is common in the United States and Europe. It is not known whether a vaccine designed to be effective against clade B would also be effective against clade C. An enhanced R&D tax credit for HIV vaccine research would not change the reality of where the commercial market lies.

Similar issues arise with malaria. A vaccine for travelers and military personnel would likely focus on the sporozoite-stage of malaria, which is the life-cycle stage of the parasite when it is first passed from a mosquito to its human host. But a vaccine focusing on sporozoites might provide only temporary protection, and thus would not be useful for residents of poor regions where malaria is widespread. In fact, such a vaccine could even be contraindicated for residents because it could weaken the limited natural immunity built up by those who survived childhood.

It might be counterproductive to attempt to overcome these problems simply by restricting the tax credits to particular forms of research—such as research on clade C HIV vaccines or malaria vaccines that target the parasite in the later merozoite stage. For example, a vaccine designed for one HIV clade might prove to be effective against other clades, or research on the sporozoite stage of the malaria parasite's life cycle might prove to be useful in creating a vaccine that would provide long-run protection. Instead of prejudging the scientific issues, it would be more effective to create rewards linked to the efficacy of a vaccine in the countries where the disease burden is greatest. Efficacy, of course, can only be assessed after a vaccine has been developed, suggesting that it may be desirable to link rewards to the final product through a pull mechanism.

Restricting an enhanced R&D tax credit to the clinical stages of research might make it easier to target populations most in need. However, it would provide a limited incentive, since only about 35 percent of the capitalized cost of R&D is incurred in the clinical phase of pharmaceutical development (PhRMA 2000b).

A third problem with an enhanced R&D tax credit is that firms would have incentives to resort to creative accounting in order to maximize their claims. Determining expenses actually qualified for a targeted tax credit would be administratively complex at best. Expenses in vaccine research may be common to a number of research projects—not all of which should qualify.[1]

Fourth, even a tax credit that could be administered effectively would only serve as an incentive for firms that have tax liabilities. Most biotechnology firms have no current profits or tax liability, and thus would not benefit unless they were permitted to pass their tax credits through to their investors—which itself would be problematic.[2]

---

[1] For example, modern vaccines typically include not only antigens (i.e., substances that elicit immune responses) that are specific to particular organisms, but also adjuvants, substances that sensitize the immune response so that less vaccine is needed to produce more antibodies. Firms would have every incentive to claim that an adjuvant intended for an ineligible vaccine was actually designed for an eligible vaccine.

[2] An alternative and more promising tax incentive would be a credit linked to the sale of an effective vaccine. Such a program was proposed by the Clinton administration. This is a pull program as it rewards research outputs rather than inputs, and is best viewed as a variant of a purchase commitment (see chapter 7).

The Contribution of Push Programs

The previous discussion does not mean that push programs are ineffective. We are currently so far away from the socially optimal level of R&D on vaccines that additional R&D, even if it involves some inefficiency, is still likely beneficial. Push programs are particularly important for basic research, which typically cannot be supported through pull programs, as we will discuss. Moreover, society has established a remarkably effective incentive system for basic research based on academic reputation and advancement. Under this system, researchers are rewarded through promotion and additional grants as well as the respect of their colleagues when they publish in highly competitive peer-reviewed journals. This has a number of advantages: scientists are free to pursue the leads that are most promising, and information is shared openly so that researchers can build on the work done by others. However, this system is less well designed for the later stages of development which often involve time consuming but not very intellectually rewarding tasks. This type of work is unlikely to get published in top journals but is nonetheless critical to the development of effective vaccines.

In the past, when there were relatively few players in pharmaceutical research outside the big pharmaceutical companies, push programs were often seen as the only game in town. However, the rise of the biotech industry, the availability of venture capital for high-risk start-ups (albeit with considerable volatility), and the increased willingness of large pharmaceutical firms to contract with universities and smaller firms have all made it much easier for researchers with reasonable prospects of developing products with an adequate market to attract outside investors. As discussed in the next section, pull programs could create such markets.

6. THE POTENTIAL ROLE OF PULL PROGRAMS

In this chapter we argue that pull programs can align incentives of researchers and funding agencies, and are particularly well suited to encouraging the later stages of vaccine development. We first will see that market size is a critical determinant of innovation. We then survey cases in which programs with pull-like features have played an important role in the development of successful vaccines. Next, we review several examples in which governments or other donors promised to reward inventors who designed a solution to a specific problem, and draw some lessons on the potential role and structure of pull programs.

THE EFFECT OF MARKET SIZE ON INNOVATION

In a seminal study, Schmookler (1966) argued that the amount of invention is governed by the size of the market and found a statistical association between R&D investments and sales. In related work on innovation in agriculture, Griliches (1957) investigated the spread of technology adoption in agriculture and found that technological change is closely linked to expected market size. Hayami and Ruttan (1971) also examined incentives for technological developments in agriculture: they concluded that agricultural technology development in the United States (where there was a high cost of labor relative to capital) was historically oriented to scale-expanding, labor-saving technologies like the cotton gin or the combine harvester. By contrast, in Japan (where both capital and land had relatively high prices relative to labor), invention was focused on investments that were labor-intensive or yield-increasing (such as improved seeds)—advances that don't require large scale to be useful.

Vernon and Grabowski (2000) investigated factors that influence the size of a pharmaceutical company's total R&D expenditures, and found a firm's expected returns to be one of the two main drivers. Scott Morton (1999) and Reiffen and Ward (2002) found positive relationships between the introduction of generic drugs and expected revenues in the target markets.

Acemoglu and Linn (2003) analyzed the effect of expected market size on the entry of new drugs and pharmaceutical innovation by examining variations in market size for pharmaceuticals linked to demographic changes. They find that a 1 percent increase in the potential market size for a drug category leads to a 4–6 percent increase in the number of new drugs in that category.

THE IMPACT OF FINANCIAL INCENTIVE PROGRAMS

Several examples reinforce the view that policies designed to increase the value of markets for pharmaceuticals can spur R&D.

The Orphan Drug Act

The U.S. Orphan Drug Act, which went into effect in 1983, creates a number of financial incentives for pharmaceutical companies to develop drugs for diseases like Huntington's, ALS (Lou Gehrig's disease), and muscular dystrophy, which affect fewer than 200,000 Americans each and therefore have a limited market.

Although the act provides for significant grants and tax credits for clinical development and testing of orphan drugs, its primary attraction for pharmaceutical companies is a promise of seven years of market exclusivity (Henkel 1999). And it seems to work: over 200 orphan drugs have been developed since 1983, while fewer than ten were introduced in the decade preceding passage of the act.

Advisory Committee on Immunization Practices and
Vaccines for Children

Vaccines for Children (VFC), a U.S. government program established in 1994, provides vaccines to needy children free of charge. The Advisory Committee on Immunization Practices (ACIP), a group of experts selected by the Department of Health and Human Services (HHS), makes recommendations to HHS regarding which vaccines should be administered in the United States. In practice, the recommendations typically set policy for immunization requirements, and also determine which vaccines will be available under the VFC.

Thus, if a vaccine is recommended by ACIP, producers of that vaccine are assured a reasonably large market. Vaccine prices are typically negotiated after the ACIP recommendation, so once ACIP has issued a recommendation, a vaccine producer is in a strong position to set the U.S. price close to the vaccine's social value. In other words, the ACIP system functions much as a pull program. If a pharmaceutical company believes that the ACIP would recommend a vaccine for a disease if one were developed, the company has significant incentive to invest in its creation. Not surprisingly, then, there has been a resurgence of interest in vaccine development aimed at the U.S. market since the creation of the ACIP.

Finkelstein (2003) investigated the private response to health policies that, in attempting to increase immunization rates, also increased the expected profits from new vaccines. In her study, she examines the introduction of various public health policies designed to increase vaccination rates against specific diseases, and estimates the change in investment in vaccines against those diseases, using changes in investment for vaccines against carefully selected diseases that were not affected by the policies to control for underlying secular trends in R&D in the vaccine market.

For example, in 1993 Medicare began covering influenza vaccinations without copayments or deductibles. This substantially enlarged the expected market for flu vaccines. The best flu vaccines in existence at the time the policy was implemented had an efficacy rate of 58 percent. Finkelstein argued that the 1993 flu policy helped stimulate the R&D responsible for the approval (in 2003) of the first new flu vaccines since 1978, as well as the first intranasal flu vaccine, FluMist, which has an 85 percent efficacy rate in healthy adults (CDC 2003). The actual benefits are sensitive to a wide variety of factors and are thus more difficult to forecast, but Finkelstein makes the case that the benefits from the 1993 flu policy (in particular, the combination of greater efficacy and wider use of the new vaccine) are likely to be tremendous, with potential annual dynamic benefits ranging from \$4.3 to \$9.5 billion.[1]

Finkelstein's estimates should be considered lower bounds on the true effects of permanent policies for three reasons. First, to the extent that these policy changes were anticipated, firms would have already been working in these areas beforehand and the before and after comparisons she relies on would underestimate the impact of the policy changes. Second, if companies did not expect the policies Finkelstein considers to last indefinitely, the impact of a policy that was clearly permanent might be greater than she estimates. Finally, to the extent that firms might interpret these decisions as indicative of a general shift toward more favorable policies for vaccines, the "benchmark" of innovation in other pharmaceuticals might itself be influenced by the policies Finkelstein examines.

While Finkelstein found a positive impact of expanding market size for flu vaccines, she argued that the spur to research is less useful to society for diseases where adequate vaccines already existed. In these cases, increasing market size merely led firms to steal market share from incumbents by introducing new vaccines that were no better than existing products.

Meningococcal C Vaccine

Beginning in 1994, the British Department of Health recorded a marked increase in group C cases of meningococcal disease, an un-

---

[1] A caveat is that sales of this intranasal flu vaccine have been lower than expected, likely at least in part due to a high pricing strategy by the manufacturer. Assuming the price eventually comes down, it is likely that a greater share of the health benefits will be realized.

common but very serious bacterial infection that can cause inflammation of membranes surrounding the brain as well as septicemia. Researchers had established that a conjugate Meningococcal C vaccine could be developed using the same technology as the Hib vaccine. The Department of Health realized that the small market size for the Meningococcal C vaccine in the United Kingdom would limit interest in the enterprise. So to stimulate commercial activity, it initiated a combination of push and pull strategies.

The Department of Health told the industry that the government would buy any effective vaccines that were made available, though it did not offer a legal guarantee (Towse and Kettler 2003). New vaccines were subsequently developed and pediatric vaccination in the United Kingdom has been routine since late 1999. Incidence of the disease in the target population has dropped by 90 percent, and Australia was sufficiently impressed by the outcome that it introduced the vaccine on a national scale.

In this case, the high level of public concern about the disease coupled with the good track record of the Department of Health created sufficient credibility to stimulate private research. But it is unclear that manufacturers would be willing to invest in R&D without legally binding commitments in cases where vaccine development was likely to take many years to reach fruition and where government priorities could easily shift.

EXAMPLES OF PULL PROGRAMS STIMULATING RESEARCH

The history of pull efforts promising specific rewards for specific products suggests that these can be a very effective tool for stimulating research. However, to work well, pull programs must be carefully constructed to make credible commitments to reward appropriate products, without committing the funder to pay for inappropriate products.

One of the earliest pull programs was established by Hiero II, king of the ancient Greek city of Syracuse. The king had ordered a new gold crown of quite precise specifications. But upon delivery, he suspected that the crown he received was not pure gold—that the goldsmith had kept some of the gold for himself and diluted the remainder with some base metal keeping the weight the same. In an attempt to uncover whether his crown was pure gold, the king gave public notice of a prize for anyone who could determine the volume of the crown. At the time, people knew no means of measuring the volume of an irregularly shaped object such as the crown. One day the famous Greek mathematician Archimedes stepped into an overly full bathtub, and realized that the volume of water that escaped the tub was exactly equal to the volume submerged in the water—meaning he could find the volume of any object simply by measuring the amount of water it displaced. Archimedes is said to have been so excited that he ran through the streets of Syracuse naked, shrieking, "Eureka! Eureka!" ("I have found it!").

In the eighteenth century, Napoleon and his government offered 12,000 francs (a fortune, at the time) to anyone who could develop a way to preserve food for the military on the battlefield or at sea. At the time, more of Napoleon's army had been killed by scurvy and malnutrition than by actual combat. After fifteen years of research, a young Parisian garnered the prize in 1809. His solution was the canning process of food preservation—partially cooking food, sealing it in bottles with tight cork stoppers, immersing the bottles in boiling water, and sufficiently heating the container (Falkman 1999).

There is a long history of prizes being offered for the solution of mathematical problems. An example is the Wolfskehl prize, which was established in 1908 to reward the first person to prove Fermat's Last Theorem, a mathematical mystery that had remained unsolved for three centuries. Initially, the prize attracted little attention from serious mathematicians, who considered the problem intractable, but did attract a large field of amateurs, none of whom succeeded. Finally, in 1997, Princeton professor Andrew Wiles succeeded in proving Fermat's Last Theorem. Of course, mathematicians work on many problems without monetary prizes, but it seems reasonable to believe that, at least at the margins, young mathematicians may focus on problems for which prizes have been offered, and that the provision of prizes raises the profile and prestige of these problems. In 2000, the Clay Mathematics Institute named seven "Millennium Prize Problems," with the solution to each carrying a $1 million prize.

In hopes of advancing aviation, in 1919 a New York hotel owner offered a $25,000 prize to the first person to fly across the Atlantic, nonstop from Paris to New York (or vice versa). Numerous pilots attempted and failed, and many thought the feat impossible. But a young twenty-five-year-old pilot set out to prove otherwise. Knowing that the long flight would require huge fuel tanks, longer wings, and a new location for the seat, Charles Lindbergh designed and supervised the construction of the *Spirit of St. Louis*. That design was, of course, successful, leading to his famous first solo flight across the Atlantic in 1927. Upon touching down in Paris, Lindbergh was mobbed by hundreds of thousands of people chanting, "Vive Lindbergh!" and his innovation sparked a public interest in flight that set the modern aviation industry on its course (Simons 2003).

The importance of credibly guaranteeing that appropriate innovation will be rewarded without committing the sponsor to pay for products that are not viable in the real world is well illustrated by two examples: the experience of the British government's prize for a method of determining longitude, and an American refrigerator prize program.

In 1707, while returning from Gibraltar to England, English navigators on a fleet of five ships misjudged the longitude and ran aground on the Scilly Isles about twenty miles from the English shore. Four of the ships sank in minutes, and over 2,000 lives were lost. The tragedy was just one of many horrific mishaps that occurred during that time because mariners lacked the ability to determine longitude while at sea. In an attempt to solve this "Longitude Problem," the British government set a prize of £20,000 for a method of determining longitude within a half a degree. The Board of Longitude expected astronomers and mathematicians to develop a solution through celestial observations of the positions and motions of heavenly bodies. In fact, the solution was developed by a humble clockmaker who developed a timepiece that was sufficiently accurate to determine time at the port of departure even on rolling ships. By comparing time at the port of departure to local time, easily ascertained in good weather by observing the sun, longitude could be determined. The inventor was rewarded, but only after a long period of tests to prove the effectiveness of the chronometer. In her popular book on the subject, Sobel (1995) argued that these delays were unnecessary, although others feel that the Board was justified in requiring these tests since a chronometer would be useless if it did not work in real-world conditions on ships subject to moisture and constant vibration.

The development of the chronometer carries several lessons. First, contests seeking to induce innovation should specify solutions and not methodologies. The chronometer solution did not fit the preconceptions of the prize-setters. Had the United Kingdom relied on push programs run by the Board of Longitude, they likely would have funded only astronomers. Second, clear conditions and the process for judging the merits of candidates should be well specified in advance.

The Super Efficient Refrigerator Program (SERP) illustrates the importance of setting specifications carefully and including a market test. In 1992, twenty-four American electricity utilities pooled $30 million to reward the first manufacturer to develop an energy-efficient refrigerator meeting certain technical specifications. SERP attracted over 500 entries from 14 manufacturers. The winner was selected largely based on technical energy efficiency considerations. Most of the prize money, however, was awarded based on a market test which paid the winner a set amount of the prize for each unit sold. Engineers were very creative in finding ways to save energy, and in the end the prize was awarded to a model that cut energy use by approximately 40 percent. However, the prize-winning unit was priced at around $1,400 (Suozzo and Nadal 1996), and used the then-unusual side-by-side design, which is reported to have been unpopular among consumers (Groseclose 2002; Sandahl et al. 1996). Consumers were unwilling to pay for the new refrigerator, and manufacturing of the product was discontinued.

In the case of the refrigerator prize, very specific technical standards for energy efficiency led to a focus on one attribute at the expense of other attributes that consumers value, such as price and design. This example illustrates the importance of making payments under a pull program subject to a market test to avoid paying for a product that won't be used. Fortunately, the SERP program did make part of the payout dependent on sales, so the sponsors did not have to pay in full for a product with little takeup. This prevented the sponsors' money from being wasted, but the overemphasis on the single criterion of energy efficiency prevented the program from fulfilling its potential in leading to the development of a new refrigerator that would be widely used. Of course, it is much easier to write technical specifications for a vaccine than for a refrigerator. Unlike refrigerators, whose market appeal depends on many factors (like style) that are difficult to specify in advance, vaccines are typically purchased by governments that make key purchase decisions based on efficacy and side effects through an established regulatory process.

Advantages and Limitations of Pull Programs

A key benefit of pull programs is that money changes hands only when a successful vaccine is developed. Funders need not worry that they will invest millions in a project that ultimately fails. Indeed, they can proceed with a commitment even if scientific opinion is divided about the feasibility of a product. Individual scientists and firms working on the problem are best placed to judge scientific prospects. If they judge scientific prospects worthwhile they can invest time and resources into pursuing projects; if not, they can invest their time and effort elsewhere. Pull programs efficiently align incentives, with governments and other funders defining the problem while private developers compete to find the best solution.

Thus, pull programs are useful in cases such as a malaria vaccine, where there exists a range of opinion on prospects for development. Funders will only provide direct push support for research when they are reasonably confident about the scientific prospects for success. As donors only pay if a product is developed under a pull program, they can make the commitment even when there is less clarity about scientific prospects. Those firms that believe the development of a malaria vaccine is scientifically feasible will then be free to pursue their research knowing there will be a market for their product if they are successful.

Well-designed pull programs can partially address the problem that some diseases have stronger advocacy groups than others. While HIV has received a large amount of political attention and support, malaria and tuberculosis have received substantially less and diseases such as schistosomiasis are all but off the radar screen of many individuals and organizations. Pull programs can help address the problem that lobby groups can make exaggerated claims about research prospects or particular diseases, because they make transparent how much society values each potential invention, separating this question from the question of technological opportunity.

Pull programs would create incentives for biotech and pharmaceutical firms to concentrate research where scientific prospects were best for vaccine development, and thus to select the most promising projects. They would also encourage researchers to focus on developing a marketable product. Many academic and government researchers have career goals and intellectual interests that orient them to fundamental science. The later, more applied stages of product development include activities that are not particularly interesting intellectually, but require considerable time and effort from highly trained scientists. Techniques for manufacturing sufficient quantities of candidate vaccines at a level of purity sufficient for clinical trials must be developed, animal models for the disease must be created, and product trials must be conducted. Nobody is likely to win a Nobel Prize for these important steps in vaccine development. But by linking payment to results, pull programs could provide strong incentives to researchers to concentrate their efforts on technology suitable for commercialization.

Pull programs offer the opportunity to harness the same energy and creativity the private sector has shown in developing products for high-income countries toward the development of products for low-income countries. It is an open, transparent approach that is difficult for special interests to capture. Private sector R&D would be attracted to worthwhile products through a market-oriented approach, and donor dollars would reward success without micro-managing the research process.

Pull programs do, however, have a number of limitations. In particular, they must specify the desired research outputs beforehand,

and coming up with the right specifications and eligibility requirements may be difficult. A pull program could not have been used to
spur the development of the Post-It Note® or the graphical user inter-
face for computers because these products could not have been ade-
quately described before they were invented. Similarly, it is usually
difficult to stimulate basic research through pull programs, since the
output of basic research is often difficult to specify in advance. It is
easier to define what is meant by a safe and efficacious vaccine, however, since existing institutions, such as the FDA, are already charged
with making these determinations. Defining eligibility standards,
even for vaccines, would still be far from a trivial matter, however, as
we shall see in a later chapter.

One of the benefits of pull (that the sponsor does not have to pay
unless and until a vaccine is developed) is also one of the potential
limitations as, without sufficient assurances, developers will be concerned that a sponsor will renege on the commitment and so not undertake the necessary research. This limitation can be overcome by
designing the commitment with sufficient credibility. This can be
achieved by, for example, having a legally binding contract with credible sponsors (see chapter 12) and by ensuring that the committee
charged with adjudicating whether technical specifications have been
met include members trusted by developers (see chapter 8).

Another issue is that pull programs could potentially lead to duplication of research activities. Of course, it is often appropriate to pursue many different leads simultaneously in searching for solutions to
important problems. For example, the organizers of the Manhattan
project wanted to create the atomic bomb as quickly as possible.
They followed several lines of research—eventually ending up with
both a plutonium bomb (nicknamed "Fat Man") and a uranium
bomb ("Little Boy").

Even when a task may seem mechanical and well-defined, it may be
useful to have multiple, competing teams, each with its own ideas on
how to execute the project. For example, the effort to sequence the
human genetic code was originally conceived as a public project that
would last fifteen years, involve thousands of researchers, and cost
around $3 billion. But at the halfway point of that time line, only 4

percent of the human genome had been sequenced. A one-time NIH neuroscience researcher had an idea for a computer methodology that could be executed more cheaply and quickly than the methods being used. And when the government was unwilling to adopt his approach, he left for the private sector—where a rough draft was completed for about one-tenth of the cost and in one-eighth the time of the original plan. This entry of the private sector spurred increased competition, as the leaders in the public program increased their pace and reoriented their research plan in an attempt to beat private enterprise to the finish line. Rather than leading to wasteful duplication, the pull incentive created by potential profit opportunities for the private sector led to a faster, cheaper, and more efficient research process that was open to new ideas.

Nonetheless, it is possible to construct theoretical examples in which pull could lead to excessive duplication of research. To illustrate this, suppose there are two promising ways to develop a vaccine. Suppose that one of them has a 60 percent chance of success and one has a 25 percent chance of success. If one assumes that investigating each lead is a totally mechanical process, so there is no benefit to having competition within a single approach, it would be efficient for one team to pursue the approach with a 60 percent chance of success, and another to try the project with a 25 percent chance of success. With push, one research team could, in theory, be centrally directed to work on each project.

However, in a decentralized system in which research is motivated by patents or other pull incentives, there may be inefficient duplication. Two teams might both pursue the approach with a 60 percent chance of success, each figuring that it would have a 30 percent chance of winning the race. In this example, the odds of success for society as a whole would have been greater if each team specialized in a different line of research.

As previously discussed, it is unclear whether replication of R&D would actually be a problem in practice. It may, in fact, make more sense for two teams to work on the most promising lead than for them to be directed to pursue different approaches. But to the extent that policymakers are confident that promising approaches are being neglected under pull programs, they could address the problem by combining push and pull.

For example, if the pull program were set at a size sufficient to encourage the more promising research approach, researchers could also be induced to work on the alternatives if they were offered an appropriate push subsidy that, together with the pull incentive, would make the project attractive.

This suggests that in some situations push and pull could be used as complementary parts of a system of R&D incentives. While both push and pull incentives are already in place for pharmaceutical products needed in high-income countries, the world lacks a pull system for diseases that primarily affect low-income countries. Chapter 7 considers several possible alternatives.

■ ■ ■ ■

7. PULL PROGRAMS: A MENU

Pull programs that reward successful drug and vaccine research could take a variety of forms. These include commitments to fully or partially financed product purchases, patent buyouts, extensions of patent rights on other products, and even best-entry research tournaments in which the quality of work is judged at a fixed date and the reward goes to the contestant closest to the goal. Governments could also signal willingness to pay more for as-yet-undeveloped vaccines by purchasing larger quantities of existing vaccines at premium prices.

Given the huge disparities between private and social returns to research, any program that committed to compensate vaccine and drug developers would likely be an improvement on the status quo. We believe, however, that committing to partially or fully financed product purchases would be most attractive.

COMMITMENTS TO FINANCE PURCHASE OF PRODUCTS AND PATENTS

Two closely related approaches are (a) committing in advance to fully or partially financed product purchases, and (b) committing to purchase the underlying patent rights.

A sponsor could guarantee a price of, say, $15 each for the first 200 million people immunized with a malaria vaccine. Alternatively, it could simply offer to pay the present value of this stream of payments, minus the manufacturing cost, in exchange for the patent rights to the vaccine. The sponsor could then place the patent in the public domain and encourage competition in manufacturing the vaccine. Both mechanisms would tie the reward to the development of a desired product and improve access to products once they had been developed.[1]

There are practical differences between the two approaches, however. Patent buyouts lead to free competition in manufacturing newly invented goods, whereas programs designed to finance purchases require the sponsor to specify more details of the goods purchased. In many cases, this implies that patent buyouts would have significant advantages over purchase commitments. For example, if a sponsor committed to purchase high-definition television sets as a way of encouraging research in the field, it would have to get involved in decisions about color, style, reliability, screen size, and other issues best left to consumers. In the case of vaccines, however, governments already purchase vaccines and regulate their quality, and thus are, in effect, the consumers. This helps mitigate the problems of purchasing products, and the problem could be further eased by requiring some sort of market test, such as the copayment requirement discussed in this chapter.

Moreover, in the case of vaccines, helping finance purchases of an actual product has significant advantages. First, because vaccines are difficult to produce, a patent buyout might leave the developer with an effective monopoly anyway. Then the public would effectively pay twice: once for the patent, and again for the product at a price far above manufacturing cost.

Second, product purchases would create a tighter link between payments and product quality. Suppose a vaccine received regulatory

---

[1] Kremer (1998) discusses the possibility of buying out patents, using an auction to establish the patent's value. This can be seen as a method of determining the appropriate cash prize in lieu of a patent. One advantage of this approach is that it can be used even for inventions such as the Post-It® note, which could not be defined ahead of time. The auction procedure described in that article may, however, be subject to collusion. For products such as vaccines, which are easier to define ahead of time and for which it is comparatively easy to evaluate effectiveness, there is no need for such an auction.

approval, but was later found to have harmful side effects—just what happened with the Wyeth-Ayerst rotavirus vaccine, which was withdrawn from the U.S. market following evidence that in rare cases it caused intussusception (a form of intestinal blockage). If the patent had been bought out at the date of regulatory approval, a wasteful legal fight might have been needed to recover the money. Vaccine purchases, on the other hand, could easily be suspended as soon as evidence of unacceptable side effects appeared.

Third, purchase commitments are likely to be more attractive politically than patent buyouts, and thus more credible to product developers. Developers are vulnerable to expropriation, even if the terms of the compensation program legally obligate the sponsor to compensate them for qualifying products. For example, a pharmaceutical firm that had just earned a windfall on a malaria vaccine might be subjected to stiff price regulation on an unrelated product.

This suggests that it is important to design a compensation program in ways that generate minimum public resentment. And purchasing malaria vaccine for, say, $15 per person immunized is likely to be more politically appealing than awarding a multi-billion-dollar prize to a pharmaceutical manufacturer.

PATENT EXTENSIONS ON OTHER PHARMACEUTICALS AS COMPENSATION FOR VACCINE DEVELOPMENT

The late Jonathan Mann, founding director of the WHO Global Program on AIDS, suggested the idea of compensating the developer of an HIV vaccine with a ten-year extension of patent rights on another pharmaceutical. With successful pharmaceuticals bringing in as much as $3.6 billion in annual sales (*CNNfn* 1998), such a patent extension would be very valuable. Moreover, patent extensions appeal to some politicians because they would not show on the government budget as an expenditure and need not run the gauntlet of the government budgeting process.

But there are drawbacks to this scheme. Patent extensions might unfairly—and inefficiently—place a disproportionate burden of the financing of vaccine and drug development on those patients who need the drug for which the patent is being extended.

Suppose an extension of the patent on Lipitor, a blockbuster anti-cholesterol medication, were promised as compensation for the development of an HIV vaccine. This would be economically equivalent to imposing a high tax on Lipitor and using the proceeds to finance cash compensation for the vaccine developer. High taxes on narrow bases are inefficient ways of raising revenue since they reduce consumption of the taxed good below the point where value at the margin equals production cost.[2] In this case, an extension of the Lipitor patent might prevent some people from getting needed treatment for heart disease. HMO's, for example, might put pressure on doctors to reduce Lipitor prescriptions if prices remained high.

Moreover, transferring rights from one product to another eliminates a key advantage of patents. A patent, after all, closely links the inventor's compensation to the value of the invention. If a product is more effective, causes fewer side effects, and is easier to administer, it will bring in more revenue. By contrast, rewarding the inventor of an HIV vaccine with the extension of the Lipitor patent would eliminate this link between the quality of the HIV vaccine and the magnitude of the compensation.

Another disadvantage of compensating product inventors with patent extensions on unrelated pharmaceuticals is that the right to extend a patent would be worth the most to firms already holding patents on commercially valuable pharmaceuticals, and these may not be the firms with the best opportunities for vaccine research. This problem would not be fully resolved by making patent extensions

[2] If governments and Health Maintenance Organizations (HMOs) purchase pharmaceuticals, patents may be equivalent to a broad-based tax. (We thank Michael Rothschild for this point.) Nonetheless, patents may still distort market allocation if HMOs and governments respond to pharmaceutical prices in their treatment decisions. Governments are less likely to do this than are HMOs, and so patent extensions are more attractive in countries with centralized health systems. Nonetheless, even under Britain's National Health Service, for example, decision-makers face internal prices. Hence, higher prices for particular drugs would lead to reduced purchases of those drugs.

tradable, since firms holding patents on commercially valuable pharmaceuticals would insist on some profit from such trades. Thus, while rewarding vaccine developers with transferable patent extension rights would be an improvement on the status quo, it would not be an ideal solution.

BEST-ENTRY TOURNAMENTS

In best-entry research tournaments, a sponsor promises a reward to whoever has progressed the furthest in research by a specific date, whether or not the goal of a useful product has been reached.[3] Best-entry tournaments are often used to select architects for large construction projects. A vaccine tournament would differ from an architecture tournament, however, because vaccine researchers could not promise a certain level of completion on a given date, whereas architects can generally submit completed designs by a deadline.

Best-entry tournaments have other limitations, too, that make them ill-suited to encouraging vaccine and drug research. A major drawback is that a payment would have to be made, no matter what amount of progress was achieved. Even if the target product proved impossible to develop, the same amount of money would be paid. Hence, best-entry tournaments may not focus effort on diseases with the best scientific prospects for success. Those interested in eradicating a particular disease will always want to encourage the establishment of best-entry tournaments for research on their disease, even if the prospects for success are low.

With a purchase program, on the other hand, no public funds are spent unless the desired product is developed. If investors realize at some point that the desired product is impossible to develop, they will choose not to throw good money after bad. This is particularly relevant for development programs that require long periods and that have very uncertain chances for success.

Another problem with best-entry tournaments is that the subjective aspects of assessing progress would open decisions to bias. For exam-

---

[3] See Taylor (1995) for a discussion of tournaments.

ple, the judges might decide to reward a firm with the most political clout, or perhaps the team that has done the most scientifically interesting work on other projects. A committee making purchase decisions for a vaccine purchase program could also be subject to bias, but there is less wiggle room in assaying a completed project. It follows that award decisions in a best-entry tournament would be more vulnerable to litigation or political lobbying after the fact.

Note, too, that best-entry tournaments would create incentives for collusion among researchers. If only a few pharmaceutical firms do a significant amount of work, they could collude to exert low effort since the reward would be paid whether or not a product was ever developed.

Best-entry tournaments may also lead researchers to put their efforts into looking good on the tournament completion date, rather than on positioning the project for a swift and successful conclusion. Firms that discover promising research leads that seem unlikely to yield solid results before the deadline might ignore these leads, while firms learning that the research lines they are pursuing are unlikely to yield a successful product might nonetheless continue their work in an attempt to hide their lack of progress.

Finally, best-entry tournaments are also politically unattractive. Governments could be embarrassed to pay large amounts for research that did not ultimately yield a valuable vaccine.

EXPANDING THE MARKET FOR EXISTING VACCINES AND DRUGS

Some observers argue that by purchasing more of existing products at higher prices, policymakers could signal their intent to provide a market for future products—thereby encouraging research on desired technologies. There are, indeed, good reasons to increase purchases of existing vaccines. But such purchases would not be an efficient means toward the end of bringing new vaccines to market.

Although the standard EPI package of vaccines is widely distributed, a number of effective vaccines that are also available are not being fully utilized.[4] Purchasing and distributing existing vaccines that are not widely enough used in low-income countries, such as *Haemophilus influenzae* b (Hib) vaccine, would be a cost-effective way to save lives and is justified in its own right, independent of any effect on research incentives.

But stimulating research on new products will require more specific incentives. It could easily take a decade to develop malaria, tuberculosis, or HIV vaccines, and developers would need to recoup their investment through sales in as many years following the vaccine roll-out. Since international interest in the health of poor countries is fickle, firms might well feel that the availability of funds to purchase vaccines now at a remunerative price would not say much about how much donors would be willing to pay for vaccines fifteen years hence. Legally binding commitments to purchase vaccines would therefore still be needed to spur research.

Moreover, paying higher prices from now on as a way to stimulate future research amounts to paying twice for the research. The Hib vaccine was developed on the basis of demand in rich countries and without any expectation of realizing substantial profits in poor countries. Increasing the price paid now would generate a windfall for the developer. Providing these extra profits might be worthwhile if it were really the only way to ensure the credibility of donors down the road. However, if it were possible to commit now to purchase future products at a remunerative price, there would be no reason to pay more for current products than developers had anticipated when they took the risk in pursuit of innovation.

Finally, some argue that increasing vaccine sales today would increase vaccine R&D budgets because pharmaceutical firms finance research on a division-by-division basis, as a percentage of current

[4] For example, the hepatitis B vaccine is underused. An effective vaccine for malaria or one of the other major killers would likely be consumed much more widely than the hepatitis B vaccine, since the disease burden of hepatitis B is small relative to that of AIDS, tuberculosis, or malaria. Moreover, malaria kills young children very quickly after infection and the onset of symptoms, whereas hepatitis B infection can remain asymptomatic for decades, and many people may not understand its relation to the deaths it causes from primary hepatic cancer in middle age or beyond.

sales. While some drug makers may use such rules of thumb to make budgetary decisions within the current R&D system, they would have a clear incentive to adjust these rules if the environment changed. In particular, an explicit, credible commitment to purchase vaccines down the road could lead these companies to invest more in developing these products. And if they did not, biotech firms, which are more flexible in their budgetary decisions, would have incentives to enter the field in response to increased market sizes.

Establishing long-term contracts would be useful both for currently available underutilized vaccines and for vaccines that are expected to be ready soon, such as rotavirus. Currently, most vaccines for low- and middle-income countries are sold on short-term contracts to buyers such as the United Nations' Children's Fund and the Pan American Health Organization. This creates uncertainty that can lead either to vaccine shortages or to unused capacity. Moreover, as discussed earlier, vaccine producers sell patented vaccines substantially above cost, and this limits the number of countries placing orders through UNICEF or PAHO. These problems could be addressed through long-term contracts, in which donors would agree to pay a relatively high price for, say, the first hundred million people immunized with a new vaccine like the rotavirus vaccine, in exchange for a commitment by the manufacturer to supply additional doses to low-income countries at a modest markup over production cost. The firm would be contractually obligated to meet demand, as long as it was given sufficient notice.

If low-income countries knew that they would have reliable access to vaccines at a modest markup, they would be more likely to add them to their immunization schedules. Both vaccine manufacturers and public health would be better served by this type of long-run contract than by the existing system of short-run contracts. Awarding these contracts to the first producers of a good vaccine would also strengthen incentives for original research since firms doing such research would not have to worry about losing market to a "me-too" product.

8. DETERMINING ELIGIBILITY

We have argued that vaccines are desperately needed for diseases primarily affecting poor countries, such as malaria, tuberculosis, and HIV, and that a vaccine commitment could prove a highly effective way of stimulating R&D on these vaccines. In the following chapters, we discuss how such a commitment could be structured—how eligibility should be judged, what price should be paid, how payments should be structured, and how the commitment could be tailored to meet the needs of different classes of sponsors.

In this chapter, we discuss eligibility. We believe that the criteria for determining which vaccines should qualify for a vaccine commitment should include: (a) technical eligibility requirements like safety, efficacy, and ease of delivery; (b) a market test of whether countries find a vaccine useful; and (c) a clause under which the commitment could lapse if the program was made obsolete by ongoing technological change or if a sufficiently long period elapsed.

BASIC TECHNICAL REQUIREMENTS

Technical requirements should include:

- *Safety.* Determined primarily by competent national regulatory authorities, for example the U.S. Food and Drug Administration (FDA).
- *Efficacy.* A vaccine commitment would need to make clear what reduction in disease incidence among vaccinated individuals would be required. It might be necessary to specify that disease

prevalence must decline for specific geographic regions and for specific age groups. The required duration of protection would also have to be specified.

- *Usability.* The utility of a vaccine in low-income-country conditions would depend on the number of doses required, the efficacy of the vaccine if an incomplete course is given, and the ages at which doses must be taken. If many doses are required, fewer children would be likely to receive the full course of immunization. If the vaccine could be given along with vaccines that are already being widely administered, delivery would be much easier.

A first step in demonstrating safety and efficacy would be for a vaccine to receive regulatory clearance by an established regulatory agency, such as the FDA or its European counterpart, the European Agency for the Evaluation of Medicinal Products (EMEA). However, since vaccines may pass risk-benefit assessments in some countries but not others, the regulatory approval process should not be restricted to the FDA or the EMEA. For example, a tuberculosis vaccine with rare side effects might not be appropriate for general use in low-prevalence countries such as the United States, but might save millions of lives in high-prevalence areas. Vaccine developers should be allowed to seek approval from other regulatory agencies in other countries.

Additional technical criteria beyond regulatory approval would be needed, since a vaccine could receive regulatory approval without being suitable for large-scale purchase for low-income countries. For example, a malaria vaccine that provided short-run malaria protection but interfered with natural immunity might receive FDA approval since it would be useful for U.S. citizens traveling to regions with malaria, who would not have built up this immunity in any case. However, it would not be appropriate for long-term residents of areas in which malaria was widespread.

Thus, vaccine developers should be required to demonstrate a minimum duration of protection before the vaccine was ruled eligible. The contract might also specify that continued eligibility would depend on demonstrating efficacy over a longer period.

A vaccine might be more effective against some strains of the disease than others, and therefore be better suited to some geographic areas or some age groups than others. Thus, the commitment might include a requirement that a product could only be purchased for a particular population if it had been shown effective for the strains of disease prevalent in that population. To this end, the contract would need to specify that the developer conduct studies in a variety of regions and with a variety of disease strains. Depending on the disease, it may also be necessary to specify whether efficacy would be measured against clinical disease in general or against severe forms of the disease.

Note, too, that it would be necessary to spell out the evidence required to document efficacy. This might include the length of time subjects would be followed to determine the duration of protection, as well as procedures for ongoing monitoring after the vaccine had been introduced.

The technical requirements should also include specifications pertaining to vaccine usability in low-income countries. For example, vaccines requiring many doses to be effective might require a special waiver for eligibility. Similarly, the commitment could include a requirement that the vaccine be storable in the same conditions as the current EPI vaccines, for example.

The technical requirements for vaccine eligibility must be stringent enough to yield effective vaccines but flexible enough to encourage promising research. Unnecessarily stringent specifications would discourage pharmaceutical firms from following promising leads. For example, it would be a mistake to require a vaccine to be 90 percent effective against all strains of the disease, since this would discourage developers from pursuing a candidate vaccine likely to yield 99 percent protection against most strains, but only 85 percent protection against others. Conversely, erring on the side of flexibility could lead to production of unusable vaccines.

INDEPENDENT ADJUDICATION COMMITTEE

An independent adjudication committee (IAC) would need to judge whether the eligibility conditions had been satisfied. The committee should (a) have some discretion to waive technical requirements other than regulatory approval; (b) monitor purchased products to ensure continuing safety and efficacy; and (c) have the power to discontinue purchase of a vaccine if it turned out to be less safe or efficacious than originally anticipated. The committee would also adjudicate whether second-generation vaccines are superior to the initial vaccine (see chapter 10). Having a committee, independent from the funder of the commitment and from other political pressures, that potential developers can trust, is key to providing the credibility needed to reassure potential investors that the commitment will not be reneged upon (see chapter 10).

To guard against rejecting useful vaccines, the IAC would have the discretion to waive technical requirements for vaccines that seemed desirable but did not meet all the technical standards. On the other hand, the adjudication committee should not have authority to impose new conditions for acceptability. Otherwise, the committee could abuse its discretion by raising standards after pharmaceutical companies have sunk investments in R&D. If post-license clinical trials are needed to ensure that purchased vaccines remain safe and efficacious, the vaccine commitment contract should specify the committee's monitoring powers and responsibilities.

An adjudication committee should be structured in a way that insulates it from political pressure and gives developers confidence that the rules would be interpreted fairly. Methods would have to be devised to assure pharmaceutical executives that adjudicators would not abuse their discretion to lower the returns on research after the fact. Once a vaccine developer had sunk hundreds of millions of dollars into R&D, adjudicators might be tempted to offer a price for the vaccine that covered only manufacturing costs or to insist on excessive product testing and improvements. This is an example of what we previously identified as a time-consistency problem.

The credibility of a vaccine commitment would be enhanced by appointing decision-makers trusted by vaccine developers and insulating them from political pressures through long-term appointments. It would also make sense to write the rules used for eligibility and pricing so as to put limits on the committee's discretion.

Looking down the road, the credibility of purchase commitments could also be enhanced by establishing a program covering a wider range of diseases that primarily affect low-income countries.[1] Such a program would be able to build a reputation for fair play and for fulfilling promises.[2] Similarly, it would help to include some long-established institutions with a reputation for being interested in furthering R&D in pharmaceuticals in the adjudication process.

The experience of central banks, like the Federal Reserve, offers lessons for the design of a vaccine commitment. Just as a vaccine commitment would have to be credible, central banks must curtail expectations of inflation by credibly promising to take tough action if prices begin to rise. Central bankers are insulated from political pressures by long tenure, and a vaccine purchase program could do the same. Appointing central bankers with strong anti-inflation credentials also helps build the banks' credibility. Similarly, including some former industry officials on the vaccine committee could increase confidence that the

---

[1] On the other hand, if the program maintained a single fund used to purchase vaccines for any of several diseases, potential vaccine developers might fear that once they had invested in vaccine research, the purchase program would try to minimize payments for the vaccine in efforts to save money to buy vaccines for other diseases. This problem could be addressed by maintaining separate funds (or making separate financial commitments) for individual diseases.

[2] The problem of inducing firms to conduct R&D on vaccines for which they expect the government to be the major purchaser is in some ways similar to the problem of inducing firms to develop weapons for which they expect governments to be the primary customer. In each case, the government must convince the firms that it will not take advantage of them by insisting on low prices once they have already sunk their investments. The U.S. Department of Defense does not instruct procurement officers to purchase equipment at the lowest possible price, but to purchase at a price that covers suppliers' costs. The formulas for calculating costs typically allow firms to cover more than manufacturing costs, which in turn provides an incentive for firms to invest in R&D to win procurement contracts. Rogerson (1994) suggests that the fact that the Defense Department has a reputation for abiding by this rule creates incentives for private investments in research that would otherwise be difficult to recover. The Defense Department has the advantage of being a long-standing institution with a reputation evolved over decades. No one, moreover, worries that the institution will be abolished down the road.

committee would not impose unreasonable conditions after a vaccine had been developed. One possibility might be to follow the procedures of an institution with a strong track record, such as the Advisory Committee on Immunization Practices, which recommends the vaccines to be given to children in the United States.[3] It also might be possible to draw on the WHO prequalification procedure, which pharmaceuticals must pass before being eligible for United Nations procurement.

Market-Test Requirement

To insure that a sponsor is not obliged to purchase vaccines that meet all the technical requirements but are still unsuitable for use in poor countries, it is important that vaccine commitments include evidence of interest from recipient countries. In this section, we consider some ways to implement a market-test requirement, as well as some safeguards against problems this requirement could create.

A country may not want a newly developed product even if it meets all preset technical requirements. For example, if a vaccine generated side effects that were medically harmless but were culturally unacceptable, people might be loath to be vaccinated. Attempts to impose its use might even backfire, increasing resistance to vaccination in general. It is difficult to anticipate all possible contingencies in which purchase of a seemingly effective vaccine would not be warranted. In particular, it is certainly appropriate for the program sponsor to agree to pay for vaccine doses only if a recipient country agrees to use the vaccine and takes the steps necessary to ensure that the product can be delivered to those who need it.

Copayments

It probably makes sense for the program sponsor to commit to cover most, but not all, of the cost of the vaccines. The recipient country—

---

[3] Organizations such as PAHO and UNICEF, which purchase existing vaccines, could face an apparent conflict of interest given their appropriate focus on achieving value for money in their current purchases. They would therefore not be the best choice as independent administrators and adjudicators of a vaccine commitment.

or a separate donor acting on its behalf—should probably also be required to make a copayment to demonstrate its commitment to the vaccination program. This would be in addition to the delivery costs which the recipient or other donors would also need to cover. In many cases, copayments would have to come from a separate donor rather than from the recipient country. But whether the country itself or an independent agency served as the cofunder, it would still provide a useful market test that someone thought the vaccine was actually useful. This would help ensure against a vaccine developer finding a way to satisfy the letter of the technical requirements without actually producing a useful product. The experience of the SERP refrigerator prize suggests this danger is not merely hypothetical.

Copayments could also boost the incentives for vaccine developers by increasing the potential returns to the vaccine producer for any given expenditure by the funder. On the other hand, copayments would necessarily add another set of decision-makers to the process. And to the extent that this added to uncertainty of whether a product would eventually be purchased, it would also increase the risk of R&D investment. This suggests that copayments should be modest.

Once a vaccine was developed, countries would face appropriate purchase incentives if the copayment equaled the cost of producing another dose at the margin. In theory, it might be possible to get countries to cover more of the costs of the program without undermining efficiency by setting the level of copayments just below the countries' estimated willingness-to-pay.[4] Since richer countries are likely to be willing to pay more than poorer countries, country copayments could be linked to per capita income.[5] Tying copayments to income also achieves many of the benefits of tiered pricing. If copayments were set appropriately, countries would have access to a vaccine if its social value exceeded marginal production costs.

---

[4] If there are substantial positive cross-border externalities of vaccine consumption, the copayment should be lower.

[5] Willingness-to-pay is also likely to be higher for countries with a greater burden of disease. But linking copayments to disease burdens seems inequitable and is likely to be unfeasible politically.

Preventing Tied Deals and Corruption with Copayments

The market test should be structured carefully to avoid creating incentives for vaccine developers to bribe potential recipient countries to accept the vaccine, or for recipients to extort side payments in exchange for agreeing to accept vaccines. For example, developers could try to induce a country to accept a low-quality vaccine by kicking back some percentage of the purchase price in the form of price reductions on other pharmaceuticals, or even bribes.[6] By the same token, health authorities in poor countries could insist on these payments as a condition of accepting a high-quality vaccine.

The vaccine commitment system could use safeguards to minimize such problems. The technical requirements for eligibility provide the first and most important line of defense, preventing a recipient country from using the program to purchase a quack product manufactured by a politically connected firm.

The problem of countries using the demand requirement to extract side payments or other favorable treatment from vaccine developers could be addressed with a separate safeguard, outlined in the next chapter, in which the program sponsor would guarantee a high price for immunizations up to some specified quantity, while obtaining a commitment to lower prices for sales beyond this amount. Under such a mechanism, a government seeking side payments would have little bargaining power in dealing with the vaccine developer, for if it threatened to reject a vaccine, the manufacturer would lose relatively little revenue at the margin.

Finally, the annual number of doses purchased for a country could be limited to the number needed for newborns, with some adjustment

---

[6] Outright corruption could be limited with provisions that punish firms offering bribes and restricting the amount of travel, training, and other perks that sellers could provide to health ministry officials. Under the U.S. Foreign Corrupt Practices Act, executives who bribe foreign governments are subject to criminal prosecution. Other nations have adopted similar laws. Since the markets for drugs and vaccines represent a small part of overall business for most large pharmaceutical companies, they would likely be reluctant to risk bad publicity, the attention of regulators, and legal sanctions.

for the initial years of the program when a backlog of vulnerable people would need to be vaccinated. This, along with the two-part pricing structure discussed previously, would limit the potential loss from inflated orders.

Exit Clauses

It may be useful to incorporate two types of exit provisions into a vaccine commitment. First, sunset provisions could allow for an exit for sponsors after a certain length of time. If thirty years pass and no substantial progress has been made on the product of interest, a vaccine commitment may not be the most useful approach, and the policy would be worth reevaluating. Thus, a sunset clause could be incorporated specifying, for example, that any time after twenty years had passed sponsors could give notice that they would let the commitment lapse after an additional ten years, if no vaccine had been developed by that point. A clause could potentially allow the sponsor to give this type of ten-year notice even earlier if no vaccine had reached phase 3 trials.

Another type of exit provision could allow for obligations to end if the disease environment changed sufficiently to obviate or radically reduce the need for the vaccine. For example, if new insecticides against the mosquitoes that transmit malaria led to the virtual elimination of malaria, and it appeared this would be permanent, it would not make sense to require a program sponsor to spend billions on a malaria vaccine, or indeed to encourage biotech and pharmaceutical firms to devote effort to the search. To deal with such contingencies, a vaccine commitment might specify that the sponsor's obligation would end if the independent adjudication committee determined that the burden of disease had fallen by more than 50 or 75 percent.

To avoid the danger that an exit option of this type would be used to renege on the commitment, it would be important to (1) vest the authority to invoke this clause with the IAC, which would be chosen for its credibility, rather than the sponsor, which might have a financial interest in the decision; (2) require a supermajority of the IAC (perhaps a three-fourths vote) to invoke such a clause; and (3) make any decision to invoke the clause subject to legal challenge.

Exit clauses would increase the risk borne by vaccine developers, but biotech and pharmaceutical firms routinely bear the risk that alternative technologies will render current approaches superfluous. There is no reason this should be any different for firms working on diseases of poor countries. Indeed, it is efficient for researchers to consider this reality when choosing avenues for research.

Removing any elements of the eligibility system would create risks. For example, not allowing the IAC to grant waivers would increase the prospect that the commitment would fail to cover a desirable vaccine. Granting the committee discretion to impose additional requirements opens the possibility that it would abuse its discretion, raising the bar facing vaccine developers after they had already sunk huge investments into R&D. Fear of this could deter investment. Not requiring recipient countries to agree to use a candidate vaccine would risk the possibility that the sponsor would be forced to purchase a vaccine that was unusable. Not including sunset provisions would risk spending billions without any added impact on needed innovation.

■ ■ ■ ■

9. HOW MUCH SHOULD WE PROMISE TO PAY FOR A VACCINE?

There are two ways to approach this issue. First, what market size is needed to spur research? Second, what is the highest price at which a vaccine would be cost-effective? Here, we analyze the total market value needed to spur research. A discussion on how pricing under a vaccine commitment should be structured is included in the next chapter.

WHAT MARKET SIZE IS NEEDED TO SPUR RESEARCH?

The larger the potential market, the more firms will enter the field, the more research leads each firm will pursue, and the faster a product is likely to be developed. The more researchers entering the field, the smaller the chance that any particular firm will be the first to develop a vaccine. This means that increasing the size of the vaccine commitment does not necessarily increase any single developer's expected profit, but does lead more firms to enter the development race. In light of the enormous burden imposed by malaria, tuberculosis, and HIV/AIDS, it is important to provide sufficient incentives for multiple researchers to enter the field so that vaccines can be developed quickly.

Here we discuss several ways of determining the appropriate market size. We argue that cost-plus pricing would be inappropriate, and that looking at statistics on R&D costs may not be appropriate either.

A better approach would be to seek to make the revenue from investments in neglected diseases comparable to that from existing commercial products.

Why not simply pay developers based on their research cost, plus a profit margin? Potential developers know their research may fail, and they must factor this possibility into their investment decisions. Specifically, if a potential developer is to pursue a line of research, it must be convinced that the reward for a successful product would at least cover the risk of failure. For example, if biotechnology investors expect that a candidate product has one chance in ten of succeeding, they would require at least a tenfold return on their investment in the case of success to make the investment worthwhile before the fact.[1] Yet, if a pull program offered a tenfold markup on research costs, a firm that felt success approaching would have every incentive to inflate its R&D cost, rather than to economize.

Another approach to estimating necessary market size is to look at the average cost of pharmaceutical development. DiMasi et al. (2003) examined sixty-eight randomly selected New Chemical Entities (NCEs) from a survey of ten pharmaceutical firms and found that, taking into account the risk of failure at each stage in the drug development process, the average capitalized cost per approved NCE was $802 million in year 2000 dollars, or $873 million in 2004 dollars. However, development costs vary widely. DiMasi et al. find that for most stages in the development process, the standard deviation of cost is greater than the mean. Vaccine trials require very large numbers of subjects, and are therefore expensive. Moreover, the cost of develop-

---

[1] As discussed previously, advocates for grant-funded research programs may have reasons to be overly optimistic about the prospects for vaccines. The Institute of Medicine estimated in 1986 that a malaria vaccine could be developed for $35 million (IOM 1986). This figure is far too low. The cost estimate seems to have assumed success at every stage of the vaccine development process. In fact, it is likely that many candidates will have to be tried before a usable vaccine is developed. A further indication that the Institute of Medicine's estimates were excessively optimistic lies in their 1986 prediction that a malaria vaccine could be licensed within 5–10 years.

ing malaria, tuberculosis, or HIV vaccines may be much higher than suggested by these estimates, since surveys of existing pharmaceuticals give disproportionate weight to the low-hanging fruit—the new chemical entities that are cheap to develop. In addition, estimates of pharmaceutical development costs are controversial. DiMasi's estimates drew fire from the consumer interest group Public Citizen, which claimed that DiMasi's study selected from a sample of the most expensive drugs, and overreported the costs of clinical trials (Public Citizen 2002). In addition, because a portion of expenditures on research and development are tax-deductible, companies may have incentives to attribute general expenditures to R&D.

Two other approaches seem more promising. The first is to use the opinion of outsiders familiar with the industry about the level of revenue needed to spur significant investment. Venture capitalists often look for peak annual market size of $500 million in making investment decisions.[2] For example, Robbins-Roth (2000) report that $500 million in peak annual sales may be sufficient to attract R&D investments. Assuming the typical product life cycle as in Grabowski et al. (2002), this corresponds to a net present value of about $3.3 billion, if one assumes a real cost of capital of 8 percent, which corresponds to long-run stock market returns. (The real cost of capital is the nominal return minus inflation, so this would correspond to an 11 percent nominal cost of capital if inflation were 3 percent).

Perhaps the most attractive approach is to look at concrete evidence on the revenue needed to induce research on pharmaceuticals. The most recent comprehensive analysis of sales revenue for pharmaceutical products is by Grabowski et al. (2002), in which the authors report on 118 NCEs introduced into the United States between 1990 and 1994.[3] Using an estimated industrywide nominal cost of capital of 11 percent,[4] the net present value (at the time of market introduction) of sales of the average product in their sample was $2.8 billion in year 2004 dollars.

[2] Personal communication with Andrew Metrick.

[3] The following discussion draws heavily on work with Ernie Berndt, Georg Weizsäcker, and Pia Bruce (2003).

[4] With 3 percent inflation, an 11 percent nominal cost of capital is equivalent to an 8 percent real cost of capital.

In thinking about the necessary value of a vaccine commitment, one may need to adjust these figures since the revenues reported by Grabowski et al. (2002) were partially spent on marketing. Under a vaccine commitment program, a potential vaccine manufacturer would need to spend considerably less on promotion. Rosenthal et al. (2002) estimate that, relative to sales, expenditures on promotion by U.S. pharmaceutical companies has remained fairly constant at about 15 percent of revenue.

After making an adjustment for lower marketing costs since firms would be selling direct to the government or to UNICEF, $2.5 billion in 2004 dollars in net present value of sales would be needed to match the average revenue brought in by NCEs. Of course the sample of existing products includes the "low-hanging" fruit of products that were easy to develop. To the extent that developing a malaria vaccine is more technologically challenging than developing the typical product, the appropriate payment would be greater. According to Grabowski et al., products between the 70th and 80th percentiles of the distribution earned an average of $3.4 billion (2004 dollars) in net present value of revenues, while those between the 80th and 90th percentiles of the distribution earned $5.5 billion in 2004 dollars. Adjusted for marketing costs, $3.0 billion in net present value of revenues would be needed to match products between the 70th and 80th percentiles and $5.0 billion would be needed to match those between the 80th and 90th percentiles (both in 2004 dollars). For our purposes here, we take $3.0 billion as our target revenue as it represents a substantial improvement over the mean revenue but does not attempt to match the top blockbuster drugs.

Of course, a vaccine developer would earn some revenues outside of the commitment program. For example, a malaria vaccine could be sold to travelers and to the military in high-income countries, to middle-income countries such as Brazil, and to the private sector in poor countries. An estimate from the popular press (Reuters 2003) suggests that the annual market for malaria prophylaxis drugs from sales to travelers and tourists from industrialized countries and the military could be as much as $200 million, but others cite much lower figures and overall this figure is very difficult to reliably predict.

At an 8 percent real cost of capital, if a vaccine captured a $100 million market in peak annual sales and the profile of sales over time followed that of a typical pharmaceutical (Grabowski et al. 2002), the net present value of those sales would be about $650 million.

Adding in $100 million of additional revenues from private sales in developing countries yields $750 million in net present value of revenues outside of the commitment program.

To generate $3.0 billion in total revenue, the program would therefore have to generate approximately $2.3 billion in sales through the program. To give some sense of pricing, under reasonable assumptions on takeup rates, this would correspond to a commitment to pay $15 in real terms for each of the first 200 million people immunized under the program. For a three-dose vaccine, this would be $5 per dose.

The price offered should be adjusted to keep pace with inflation, since it is uncertain how long it would take to develop a vaccine. If the price were constant in nominal terms, then the total real value of sales would decrease if the vaccine took longer to develop—which would be perverse, given that a scientifically challenging vaccine would require if anything more, not less, encouragement to develop. A commitment of $15 per person immunized in today's dollars would correspond to about $20 ten years from now, assuming 3 percent inflation.

COST-EFFECTIVENESS: WHAT IS A VACCINE WORTH?

A vaccine commitment should be large enough to motivate research. But it should not be so expensive that alternative health interventions could save more lives with the same resources. In this section we first show that once a vaccine is developed, purchasing and delivering it at the agreed price would be highly cost-effective compared to other health interventions. Then we attempt to evaluate the wider impact of the program—namely, its likely effect on speeding up the development and distribution of a vaccine. We argue that a commitment is likely to substantially advance vaccine development and to speed access to poor countries once a vaccine is developed, and that even if the commitment accelerates the date of development and distribution by relatively modest amounts, it would be a very worthwhile policy.

We noted earlier that the World Bank's 1993 World Development Report treated health interventions that cost less than $100 per year of life saved in poor countries as cost-effective, while more recently a country's per-capita GNP has been used as an appropriate benchmark (GAVI 2004; WHO 2000d). Currently, a variety of health interventions are financed in low-income countries, and their cost-effectiveness varies widely. The cluster of vaccines against polio, diphtheria, tetanus, and pertussis that are routinely given through the standard EPI package of childhood vaccines, for example, is estimated to cost no more than $20 in low-income countries and $40 in middle-income countries for every DALY saved (Jamison et al. 1993). Of course, this estimate is for the average cost, and it is important to note that the marginal cost of extending coverage to more remote populations is likely much greater due to the need to develop and extend health infrastructures. Estimates of the cost of antiretroviral treatment per year of life saved are sensitive to assumptions about the cost of delivery and the epidemiological effects of treatment (which could be either positive or negative, depending on behavioral response), but the 2001 call by 133 Harvard faculty members for antiretroviral treatment (Adams et al. 2001) estimated that purchasing and delivering antiretrovirals using a DOTS approach would cost $1,100 per year. As discussed earlier, their analysis assumed an average cost of $650 per patient per year for costs of the antiretrovirals. Adjusting their analysis for even the lowest of the recently negotiated estimates of antiretroviral costs, $140 per year (McNeil 2004), suggests a cost per year of treatment of approximately $613.

Overall, $100 per extra year of life can be taken as a conservative cutoff for programs that are clearly cost-effective and to give some sense of magnitudes. If aid expenditures cost less than this per year of life saved, it seems unlikely that more lives would have been spared if the same funds had been spent in other ways. At higher costs per DALY, the case is less clear.

It is useful to consider the cost-effectiveness of a commitment to purchase a malaria vaccine at a price of $15 per person immunized (in 2004 dollars) for the first 200 million people immunized conditional on the supplier agreeing to a price of $1 per person (which is still more than the current price of many EPI vaccines) thereafter. The exact cost-effectiveness of such a commitment depends on a variety of assumptions.[5] But to get an idea of the magnitudes, consider a case in which (a) the contract covered all countries with a GNP of less than $1,000 per year with sufficient disease prevalence to make vaccination worthwhile; (b) countries adopted the vaccine over seven years and eventually attained a steady-state immunization level five percentage points above those currently attained under the EPI program; (c) the vaccine required three doses but could be delivered with the EPI package at an additional per person cost of $0.75; and (d) the vaccine was 60 percent effective and protected against infection for 5 years and did not lead to a rebound effect by weakening natural limited immunity. Given these assumptions and data on population, fertility, and disease prevalence, we estimate the number of people that would be vaccinated in each country each year, the DALY burden of disease per person in each country, and the health benefits that would accrue in each year as a result of vaccination. Under these assumptions, the cost—including incremental delivery costs—per discounted DALY saved would be about $15 (in 2004 dollars). Under similar assumptions, a commitment to guarantee a price of $15 per person immunized for the first 200 million people immunized against HIV or tuberculosis would also be highly cost-effective.

These calculations are likely too pessimistic. They do not include epidemiological benefits—vaccinating a significant fraction of the population may slow the spread of a disease, and thus benefits may spill over to the unvaccinated. They also do not include health benefits to people in middle- and high-income countries, or benefits to adults in low-income countries who purchase a vaccine privately. They assume that the vaccine would be given randomly throughout a

---

[5] A more detailed description of our data and assumptions on burden of disease, fertility, delivery costs, and the benefits of vaccination can be found online at http://post.economics.harvard.edu/faculty/kremer/.

country and thus do not factor in any benefits of targeting vaccine delivery within countries to areas that have the most severe disease problems. Finally, they do not include the benefits of increasing vaccination rates for other diseases that might result from parents bringing their children in to clinics to vaccinate them against malaria.

It is thus clear that purchases under a vaccine commitment would save more lives than almost any alternative use of funds. Indeed, commitments would remain cost-effective under a wide range of assumptions about vaccine efficacy, level and speed of vaccine adoption, and the amount of money spent for vaccines.

A user-friendly interactive program calculating the cost-effectiveness under different scenarios can be accessed online at http://post .economics.harvard.edu/faculty/kremer/. This interactive program can be used to demonstrate that a vaccine commitment remains cost-effective even when many of the assumptions in the base case are varied. This sensitivity analysis can also inform us about the key technical criteria to be included in a contract by highlighting which characteristics of a vaccine are important for ensuring cost-effectiveness.

The cost-effectiveness of the vaccine is not very sensitive to changes in assumptions about efficacy, takeup rates, or the price offered. For instance, a malaria vaccine that was only 50 percent effective would still cost less than $20 per DALY saved as of the time of vaccine development. Even if the phase-in of vaccine adoption takes fifteen years and adoption only ever reaches a plateau 10 percentage points below the 2002 DTP3 rates, the program would still cost less than $20 per DALY saved and generate $1.9 billion in net present value (NPV) of revenue for pharmaceutical companies (in 2004 dollars). Including the private market for the vaccine in low- and middle-income countries, as well as travelers and military markets in richer countries, the total revenue would still reach $2.5 billion, the average NPV of revenue for existing pharmaceutical products.

A vaccine commitment would also be cost-effective at the time of vaccine development under a wide range of contract provisions. To be comparable to drugs falling between the 80th and 90th percentiles of the revenue distribution, and generate $5 billion in net present value of sales on average, a commitment could offer $25 per person immunized for the first 225 million people immunized. This would cost about $21 per DALY saved. As discussed below, if it sped vaccine development by even three years, this higher commitment might prove more attractive than a smaller commitment of $15 per person for the first 200 million people immunized.

Cost-effectiveness is more sensitive to assumptions about the number of doses required and the duration of protection. Even vaccines with relatively low efficacy will be cost-effective if they can be delivered with the current (three-dose) EPI vaccine package. This is because adding an additional vaccine to this package is relatively cheap. We have assumed a $0.75 incremental cost of adding a three-dose vaccine to the EPI package, although even at several multiples of this the delivery would be quite cheap. In contrast, delivery outside the EPI schedule would be expensive (we have assumed a cost of $5 per dose).[6] To illustrate, adding two doses outside of the EPI schedule would bring the cost per DALY to about $25 and nationwide delivery would likely only be cost-effective in African countries, which have the highest burden of malaria.[7]

Similarly, cost-effectiveness is sensitive to changing assumptions about duration of protection. As malaria primarily kills children under the age of five who have not yet gained natural immunity, the cost per DALY increases rapidly for vaccines that provide less than five years of protection. If a vaccine provided only two years of protection, the cost per DALY saved would rise to $26. This could fall if people could be re-vaccinated, but this would depend on how often boosters were needed. A vaccine commitment for malaria should take these considerations into account when specifying technical requirements.

The previous calculations demonstrate that, once a vaccine meeting appropriate technical requirements is developed, purchasing it at the agreed price will be one of the most cost-effective health interventions conceivable. There is no reason to fear, therefore, that a vaccine com-

---

[6] Delivery costs for the EPI vaccines, which include three contacts, are estimated at $15.

[7] In our calculations we assume that countries drop out of the program if delivery costs exceed $100 per DALY saved.

mitment would tie donors to future purchases that would not, when the time came, be one of the most effective ways to save as many lives as possible for a given budget. We now examine a somewhat more complex issue—the value of the commitment in accelerating the development and distribution of a vaccine. To assess this, we need to make assumptions about what would have happened in the absence of a commitment.

In the absence of a price commitment, both development and adoption of the vaccine could be delayed. It is difficult to know how much a vaccine commitment would speed vaccine development, but one indication that the effect is likely to be substantial comes from the Orphan Drug Act. As noted earlier, while fewer than ten new orphan drugs were discovered in the decade prior to the 1983 passage of the Orphan Drug Act, more than 200 were discovered since then. A vaccine commitment is also likely to substantially accelerate access in the poorest countries. As noted earlier, when the hepatitis B vaccine was introduced at $30 per dose, it was rarely used in low-income countries (Muraskin 1995; Galambos 1995). The historical record suggests adoption of new vaccines in developing countries could easily be delayed by ten to fifteen years in the absence of a commitment.[8] The health benefits of speeding development of a malaria vaccine would be tremendous, since the disease kills a million people each year.

---

[8] We estimate delays in access based on the historical record, but one could argue that donors are now more willing to spend on vaccines. However, if one believes that even in the absence of a commitment, donors would immediately buy a vaccine and distribute it at a price comparable to the initial price offered under the vaccine commitment, then the cost of purchasing and distributing the vaccine would be the same with or without a vaccine commitment, and any benefits of accelerated development associated with announcing a commitment in advance would be without cost. If the money is going to be spent on the vaccine anyway, clearly it is more cost-effective to reap the benefits of faster development by announcing this policy in advance and entering into a vaccine commitment. Conversely, if one believes that companies would have to give away a vaccine in poor countries at production cost, it is difficult to argue that a vaccine commitment would not be critical in providing a financial incentive to advance vaccine development.

If a vaccine commitment advanced vaccine development by ten years and accelerated access in poor countries by ten years, it would still cost only about $23 per additional DALY saved. Even in the extreme case in which a price commitment sped up vaccine development by only one year and adoption in poor countries by only two years, the program would cost about $80–$90 per additional DALY saved—still less than the $100 per DALY threshold for the most cost-effective interventions.

By a similar line of reasoning, if increases in the size of the commitment would accelerate development of a vaccine, it may be worthwhile to undertake a larger commitment. Paying $25 per person for the first 225 million people immunized rather than $15 per person for the first 200 million people would meet the average net present value of products between the 80th and 90th percentiles of existing commercial products. The larger commitment would cost less than $100 per additional DALY saved if it advanced development by only three years relative to the smaller commitment.

There is a range of values under which a vaccine commitment would be sufficient to stimulate substantial research, yet still be extremely cost-effective. A commitment of $15–25 per person immunized for the first 200–250 million people immunized would certainly be appropriate. The larger the commitment, the more firms will enter the search for a vaccine, and the faster a vaccine is likely to be developed. Since malaria kills 3,000 people every day, erring on the side of parsimony does not seem wise.

10. HOW SHOULD PAYMENT BE STRUCTURED?

In this section we begin by arguing that, once the overall level of compensation for vaccine developers is set, the program should be structured to cover as many people as possible. Since manufacturing costs are likely to be low, vaccine developers would care primarily about total revenue. But public health benefits would be far greater from covering more people at a moderate average price per person rather than fewer at a higher price. One attractive option would be to guarantee a relatively high price for some initial number immunized in exchange for a commitment to lower prices thereafter.

We then consider how the program should be structured to respond if multiple vaccines for the same illness were developed. Finally, we consider the possibilities of paying bonuses based on product quality and of modifying the commitment if the initial reward offered proved insufficient.

As discussed earlier, the key determinant of research incentives is the present value of the expected revenue generated by a product. This follows from the fact that, with pharmaceutical development, the fixed costs associated with research and development are high while the marginal cost of producing an additional dose is relatively low.

One implication: as a first approximation, prices would best be set per person immunized or treated, not per dose. There is no reason to pay more if multiple doses are required to provide immunity than if only a single dose is required. In fact, a vaccine is more valuable if a single dose provides immunity, as this would reduce delivery costs and would increase the number of people who completed the vaccination regimen.

A second implication is that the program would not save money by excluding large countries from coverage or by excluding countries where vaccination is cost-effective at the marginal cost of vaccine manufacture—but not at the average price paid for vaccination under the program. Limiting coverage this way would be a false economy because, if fewer doses were purchased, the guaranteed payment price per person immunized would have to be greater to induce the same amount of research.

On the other hand, if some buyers would have bought vaccines in the absence of a program at prices greater than or equal to the price paid by the program, requiring these populations to be covered would reduce incentives to develop vaccines. Thus, while a vaccine commitment should cover all low-income countries, it should leave manufacturers free to sell in high-income countries at whatever prices they can negotiate. It is unclear whether middle-income countries, such as Brazil, should be covered.

One attractive approach may be first to decide on the sum needed to spur research and then to pay this out by offering a relatively high price per person immunized until a certain level of total payments is reached. For example, the sponsor could guarantee $15 per person immunized (in 2004 dollars), subject to a 10 percent copayment, for the first 200 million children immunized against malaria in areas where the disease is prevalent. The exact net present value of such a commitment would depend on how quickly the malaria vaccine was developed, but a reasonable estimate would be $2.3 billion in 2004 dollars.[1] Provisions would also be needed to ensure that payments were only made for sales of vaccines that could reasonably be expected to be delivered to those at risk.

---

[1] The $2.3 billion estimate was calculated under the assumption that adoption of the vaccine would eventually reach the 2001 DTP3 rates. The calculation assumes that it takes seven years to reach the steady state and that rates of adoption in the transition years increase linearly.

Thereafter, developers could be required to make the vaccine available at a moderate margin over the cost of production. This could be enforced by requiring the developer to grant the program sponsor a restricted license to manufacture the vaccine and sell it in the poorest countries. As long as the developer continued to supply the vaccine at reasonable cost, the sponsor would not use the license. The contract could include a clause penalizing the provider if the firm did not deliver a specified quantity of the vaccine.

One major practical advantage to guaranteeing a high price for the first people immunized, subject to copayments, as opposed to committing to a specific schedule of purchases, is that it is difficult to predict how much vaccine countries will want and will be able to distribute. This will depend on a host of vaccine characteristics, as well as on the political salience of vaccines far in the future. Although it may seem obvious that ministries of health should move rapidly to adopt a vaccine, political pressure within countries may be just as high or higher for treatment of people who are already ill or for other activities, such as funding health worker salaries. Ministries may be reluctant to rearrange vaccination schedules or to reassign health workers, and may prefer to let other countries go first to see if there are unanticipated side effects.

As noted earlier, from the standpoint of vaccine developers, one disadvantage of a system of copayments is that developers bear the risk that demand will be weak. However, this is a risk that pharmaceutical companies take with other products, and it would not make sense for the sponsor to bear all this risk. For then, a developer that knew the product was unlikely to be used widely might press ahead with an unsuitable vaccine. In addition to adopting a two-part pricing structure, one way of sharing the risk of slow diffusion would be for the sponsor to undertake the financing of some activities designed to encourage early adoption of the new vaccine by national health authorities.

If a system that required copayments proved completely unacceptable to potential vaccine developers, it might be possible to consider a hybrid system. A hybrid contract could be structured as follows: any firm meeting the base technical specifications, as adjudicated by the

IAC, would qualify for the price guarantee, subject to copayments. To qualify for a commitment that would not be conditional on copayments, however, the vaccine would have to reach a higher level of technical specifications. The IAC would also have to certify that the vaccine was practical in low-income country conditions and that the need for the vaccine had not been substantially reduced by other technological developments.

PAYING FOR MULTIPLE VACCINES AND MARKET EXCLUSIVITY

The rules for a vaccine commitment would need to cover the case in which more than one vaccine is developed. The rules should be set with three objectives in mind: (1) fashioning incentives to appropriately reward development of the initial vaccine; (2) creating incentives to improve on the original vaccine; (3) delivering the best available vaccines to patients. A variety of options are available, ranging from a pure-winner-take-all system to a system in which any licensed product could compete for sales and the program would simply reward products in proportion to their sales. This section addresses the question of how to balance these objectives.

Rewards to individual developers should ideally reflect the value of each vaccine to society. This means that the first adequate vaccine should be rewarded more than subsequent vaccines. Once an adequate vaccine is developed, the incremental benefit of the second vaccine typically will be smaller. For example, society would benefit much more by going from no vaccine to a 70 percent effective vaccine than by going from a 70 percent effective vaccine to an 85 percent effective vaccine. This suggests that a smaller reward would bring private incentives for a second vaccine into line with its social value.

A key danger to avoid in any vaccine commitment is undermining incentives for initial R&D by offering favorable treatment to subsequent products. Once a vaccine for a disease has been developed, it often becomes easier for competitors to develop alternatives. This is true even if the first is protected by patents, as it is often possible to design "me-too" products that skirt intellectual property protection. Developers of the initial product therefore face a risk that a copycat vaccine would be produced and that this subsequent product would capture much of the market. This risk may deter the research needed to produce the first product.

This suggests that R&D on subsequent vaccines should only be rewarded if it leads to products with some superior characteristics. Research and development consumes resources, and from society's point of view it is at best a waste to divert scientific talent and equipment to vaccines that are no better than existing ones. At worst the anticipation that society might encourage the development of subsequent vaccines could actually discourage initial innovation.[2]

An attractive way to provide a larger reward to the first developer than to subsequent developers, while still preserving incentives for product improvement, is to guarantee market exclusivity to the first product unless superior vaccines are later created. This is the approach taken by the U.S. Orphan Drug Act. It is widely believed that the act's market-exclusivity provision greatly increased research on orphan drugs (Shulman and Manocchia 1997) by discouraging the development of "me-too" alternatives. In practice, showing that a subsequent vaccine is clinically superior may be difficult unless it is a significant improvement.

One potential objection to incorporating a market-exclusivity provision in a vaccine commitment is that if several developers are working on a vaccine at the same time it could increase the risk borne by developers, and thereby deter research. In the absence of a market-exclusivity clause, several firms developing comparable vaccines around

---

[2] Vaccine purchasers often prefer to have many suppliers in the market to hold down prices. However, long-term contracts can also ensure that prices are kept at reasonable levels and do not wastefully encourage the development of me-too drugs. For example, the vaccine commitment could include a provision requiring that after a certain sum had been paid to the developer, it would be required to license production for sales in poor countries. If the developer chose not to sell to low-income countries at a price near manufacturing cost, the sponsor could use the license to bring in competition. This would avoid creating incentives for wasteful R&D designed solely to circumvent the existing patent.

the same time would share the market. Providing market exclusivity to the first vaccine developer could increase risk, because the loser of the race would get nothing even if a second vaccine came to market a few months later.

Offsetting this risk, however, is the fact that the overall return to firms investing in vaccines is likely to be greater with a market exclusivity clause. If me-too products are developed, firms may dissipate potential profits in marketing expenditures. Even if the price paid through the vaccine commitment program is guaranteed, firms may engage in price competition in other markets, such as the market for a traveler's vaccine for malaria. The success of the Orphan Drug Act in increasing R&D suggests that, on balance, market exclusivity attracts developers.

If it were nonetheless thought important to share rewards with firms that narrowly lost the race to develop a vaccine, market exclusivity under the program could be shared by multiple products invented within some narrow window (perhaps a year or two) after the licensing of the first acceptable product, as well as by subsequent products that proved clinically superior for some populations. This would reduce risk for firms engaged in a tight race to develop a product, while also reducing the chance that me-too vaccines would greatly reduce sales for the initial developer and thus deter research.

If superior vaccines are produced, they should be eligible for coverage under the program. This leaves open the question of how to split compensation between the first vaccine developer and subsequent developers. One possibility would be to give the IAC discretion to split payments for subsequent vaccines between the original and subsequent developer, depending on its assessment of the incremental improvement created by the subsequent product and on the extent to which the subsequent product relied on the R&D undertaken by the first producer.

Economic theory suggests that the reward for a clinically superior subsequent vaccine would ideally be related to its incremental improvement over the original, and that the original developers should continue to receive compensation in line with the social value of their work, even if their work stimulates further advances that lead to even better vaccines. While this approach would match private and social research incentives more closely than the blanket exception for superior products in the Orphan Drug Act, it might be difficult to administer.

A simpler option to preserve rewards for the first developer would be to guarantee a high price initially and then to move to lower prices after a certain number of people had been immunized. Holding constant the expected present value paid over the entire program duration, this pricing rule would give a strong incentive to develop an appropriate product quickly—and then to sell as much as possible at the higher initial price.

This pricing rule would also help to match private returns with the social value of vaccines. The value of the incentive for the first developer would depend on the interval until superior products were available. The development of the first vaccines is most important to society if there are no other products in the pipeline. In contrast, under a winner-take-all system, there would be no differentiation in incentives for the first developer between the case in which superior products were expected soon and cases where no superior products are anticipated.

Bonus Payments Based on Product Quality

Guaranteeing a minimum price for vaccines that meet the technical requirements would help to provide a credible commitment. However, it would be desirable for developers to have incentives to create vaccines that exceeded the minimum eligibility threshold. The provisions just discussed for superior vaccines would create some incentives to develop high-quality vaccines. But one could also envision bonus payments keyed to quality. For example, bonuses could be offered for an oral rather than injectable vaccine, for vaccines that required fewer doses to be effective, or for vaccines that could be delivered as part of the Expanded Program on Immunization (EPI).

As we will discuss, varying payments with product quality would have some advantages, but it would make the process more complex. And it might create opportunities for abuse of authority by the adjudication committee, thereby increasing uncertainty for potential developers and for program sponsors.

Bonus payments could be set in either of two ways. A committee could be free to base bonuses directly on its estimates of the number of lives or DALYs saved by a particular product, estimating these quantities any way it wished.[3] Alternatively, a schedule of bonus payments could be set in advance as a function of more easily measured product characteristics, such as efficacy in clinical trials, or the number of doses needed, among others.

One advantage of paying based on lives saved is that it would encourage developers to design vaccines appropriate for actual health systems, not for some ideal. For example, if health ministries cannot deliver multiple dosage vaccines, developers would have incentives to focus on single-dose vaccines. The danger in paying vaccine developers based on realized DALYs saved is that health ministries could try to extract concessions from the developer in exchange for agreeing to distribute the product efficiently. And if developers anticipated this, they might be reluctant to invest in the first place.

[3] Information on DALYs saved might become available only gradually. For example, it may initially be unclear whether a vaccine provides protection indefinitely or only temporarily. The extent to which a vaccine prevents secondary infections might also be difficult to predict in advance. Initial bonus payments to developers could be based on conservative estimates of DALYs saved and additional payments could be made later, depending on the realization of benefits. Of course, if payments were delayed, accumulated interest would have to be paid as well. Basing bonus payments to developers on realized DALYs or lives saved, rather than on the results of the clinical trials required for regulatory approval, would create better incentives to develop products that work in the real world, rather than only in clinical trials where it is easier to make sure that delivery protocols are followed. Moreover, if bonus payments could be claimed after a product had already been used, it would be much more difficult for a price-setting committee within the vaccine purchase program to refuse to pay a remunerative price. Before a product is used in the field, the committee could argue that it deserved only a small bonus, citing potential problems. However, if the product were used, and, for example, reduced the burden of malaria by 90 percent, it would be very hard for the committee to argue that it was ineffective. (Exceptions to this are new diseases, such as HIV, for which predictions of prevalence in the absence of a vaccine are likely to be particularly inaccurate.)

Bonus payments based purely on technical criteria, such as the number of required doses or the efficacy of the vaccine, would not be subject to this problem. But there still might be room for controversy—for example, disagreement over how efficacy is measured. Whereas a system of finely tuned bonus payments might be desirable in a better world, it would likely be difficult to deploy. To the extent that potential program sponsors seek to limit their financial obligations, while vaccine developers are nervous about the adjudication committee taking advantage of them after they have sunk R&D investments, bonus payments may increase the perceived cost to sponsors without corresponding increases in the perceived reward to vaccine developers. As discussed earlier, an alternative way to provide incentives to develop superior products is to offer to buy the best one available.

Increasing the Promised Price over Time

If a vaccine commitment started at a relatively modest level and led to little research, the sponsor or other potential donors could increase the promised price. If sufficient research were still not forthcoming, they could raise the price again. This procedure mimics auctions, which are typically efficient procurement mechanisms in situations where production costs are unknown.[4]

As long as the price promised for a vaccine did not increase faster than the interest rate, firms would not have an incentive to sit on a product they have already created. A firm that delayed selling a product would postpone its returns, and therefore would have to discount these returns at an interest rate that reflected its cost of capital. Even if the price rose somewhat faster than the interest rate, it is unlikely that a firm would seek to delay the release of a vaccine, given the risk

[4] Another option would be to announce that if no vaccine had been developed by a certain date, the price would increase automatically. However, it is probably better to let future decision-makers choose whether to increase the price, since in some scenarios it would be optimal to hold the line. For example, there would be no need to increase the price if general technological advances in biology reduced the expected cost of developing a vaccine sufficiently to induce many firms to pursue vaccines.

that a competitor could introduce an alternative and the fact that if the developer has already taken out a patent, delay uses up the patent life.

Kremer (2001b) uses techniques from the economic theory of auctions to show that if there are many competing firms, a system in which the price starts low and rises over time will generate a product at close to the lowest possible cost. The greater the initial price, the more rapidly a vaccine or drug will be developed. Increasing the rate of the price increase would speed development unless very few firms could compete to develop the product.

Sponsors might want to put in place a system of monitoring how much research was being undertaken on the vaccine to inform their decision about whether a rise in price was needed. This could be done by requiring companies undertaking research on the vaccine to register with the adjudication committee and provide periodic updates to be eligible for the guaranteed price. They could, for example, be required to register before undertaking phase 1 trials of the vaccine as a condition for receiving the guaranteed payment later. Inducements to register could also include the possibility of meeting with the adjudication committee to discuss how eligibility rules would be implemented and how the committee might look on requests for waivers of certain technical specifications. The IAC would be required to treat information received from companies as confidential.

Avoiding Windfalls

The sponsor of a pull program might worry about creating a windfall for a vaccine developer that had already received sufficient push funding and was close to developing a vaccine. If so, the sponsor of a pull program might specify that if push funding had been allocated before the announcement of the pull program, the winner might be required to use some of any pull revenue to repay part or all of the push funds it had received. On the other hand, if push funding is allocated after a pull program is announced, it should be up to the push funder to decide whether to make its funding conditional on recipients agreeing to share any future profits from the sales under the pull program.

Similarly, a sponsor might feel that if a product is already more advanced at the time the pull program is announced, fewer resources would be needed to incentivize the remaining research and development needed on the product. The sponsor might therefore specify a different schedule of payments for products that had already reached phase II or phase III trials before the commencement of the pull program.

INDUSTRY CONSULTATIONS

A critical step in designing a commitment will be consultations with industry, and discussions with pharmaceutical executives about whether and how a purchase program could serve as an effective incentive for research will be extremely valuable. However, several factors should be kept in mind in interpreting the results of these conversations. First, some companies, especially larger firms concerned about public relations, may be reluctant to admit that financial considerations play a role in their R&D decisions regarding products needed in developing countries. Pharmaceutical makers have been criticized for failing to invest in research on vaccines for diseases that kill millions, while investing in more lucrative drugs (Silverstein 1999). This may make executives reluctant to admit that they are not investing in vaccines because they think the investment won't be sufficiently profitable. It is more acceptable in political terms for them to say that they are not investing because the scientific prospects for developing a vaccine are dim.

Second, as discussed earlier, questions about how large a commitment would be required for firms to invest may not be well posed. Firms must decide not merely whether to invest in developing a particular product, but also at what level to invest. The more lucrative a market, the more leads developers will pursue.

Third, pharmaceutical executives may see questions about price as part of a negotiation, and may therefore inflate their estimates—particularly if they expect that their request will be cut back later.

Fourth, pharmaceutical firms may well request programs that increase their profits without increasing their incentives to develop a new product. In particular, executives may claim that the most useful motivator would be higher prices on existing vaccines. They clearly have an incentive to argue for higher prices on existing products, whether or not this would actually lead them to invest more elsewhere.

Finally, scientists working on vaccines or drugs keyed to the needs of poor countries may not have even considered the possibility of starting biotech firms or seeking investors. If, however, a large market were expected for such products, they might turn in this direction. Since they probably have not spent much time thinking about these challenges yet, their responses to questions may not be an accurate guide to their later behavior. This makes it important to look at the historical track record of how firms have responded to incentives, as, for example in Acemoglu and Linn (2003) or Finkelstein (2003).

Fifth, firms are heterogeneous. In many cases, small biotech companies take on research at an early stage, and then, if initial tests are promising, license technology to large pharmaceutical firms which take it through further development. Pharmaceutical firms may require larger market opportunities to shift their corporate strategies. Biotech firms may be willing to enter smaller markets. Kettler (1999), for example, points to the enthusiastic response of biotech companies (compared to big pharma) to the orphan drug incentives. Similarly, some pharmaceutical firms may be more ready than others to take on vaccine projects. Averaging the responses of firms with varying inclinations does not provide a correct answer to the question of what market size is necessary to redirect efforts toward, say, a malaria vaccine. What is relevant is the marginal cost of inducing each successive firm to enter the market. For products that are at an early stage, it may be most appropriate to think of initially attracting biotech firms, which would later sell technology to larger firms.

11. SCOPE OF THE COMMITMENT

This book has discussed the rationale and design of vaccine commitments. But a similar approach might be used to induce R&D for other products, ranging from drugs to disease-resistant crops. Here, we discuss the potential for vaccine commitments against other diseases affecting low-income countries and then discuss the potential for using guarantees to encourage R&D on drugs, other medical technologies, and more efficient agricultural technologies in the tropics.

What Diseases to Cover?

Given a sufficient budget, a commitment could cover vaccines for any of a large number of diseases. Table 2 shows the number of deaths caused annually by diseases primarily affecting low-income countries, for which vaccines are needed.

One approach to selecting products to target would be to focus on the vaccines against diseases that kill the most people, that are most concentrated in poor countries, and for which market failures are the greatest. An alternative would be to start with some easier-to-develop vaccines as a way of building the credibility of vaccine commitments and learning how to improve their efficiency. As more is learned about this approach, additional pledges could be solicited to extend the program to other diseases.

Vaccines, Drugs, and Other Technologies

Commitments could potentially extend beyond vaccines to other techniques for fighting disease, including drugs, diagnostic devices,

TABLE 2

Deaths from Diseases for Which Vaccines Are Needed

Diseases	Deaths[a]	Percent
AIDS	2,285,000	27.47
Tuberculosis	1,498,000	18.01
Malaria	1,110,000	13.34
Pneumococcus[b]	1,100,000	13.22
Rotavirus[c]	800,000	9.62
Shigella	600,000	7.21
Enterotoxic E. coli	500,000	6.01
Respiratory syncytial virus	160,000	1.92
Schistosomiasis	150,000	1.80
Leishmaniasis	42,000	0.50
Trympanosomiasis	40,000	0.48
Chagas disease	17,000	0.20
Dengue	15,000	0.18
Leprosy	2,000	0.02
Total deaths	8,319,000	100.00

Notes: [a] Estimated, World Health Report (WHO 1999).

[b] A pneumococcus vaccine was approved in 2000 for use in the United States, but it needs to be tested in low-income countries, and perhaps modified.

[c] GSK and Merck have vaccines in phase-3 trials.

Source: Children's Vaccine Initiative, *CVI Forum* 18, July 1999, p. 6.

and insecticides against disease-carrying mosquitoes. The advantage of covering a range of technologies is that it would avoid biasing research toward vaccines at the expense of alternative disease-fighting approaches.

The example we discussed of the British government's eighteenth-century prize for a method of determining longitude suggests that terms should be set so as to admit a variety of solutions. Most of the scientific community believed that longitude could best be determined through astronomical observations, but the winning solution relied on the development of a more accurate clock.

However, pull programs can only be used effectively if it is possible to specify the goal in advance, and the ease with which this can be done varies among technologies. For example, it would be difficult to reward developers of new HIV/AIDS counseling techniques. It is unclear how one would establish the efficacy of such programs, the potential for using them with different populations, and the practicality of scaling them up. An adjudication committee could easily become tied up in disputes over the impact of such programs.

On the other hand, existing institutions such as the FDA or EMEA already have credibility in determining the safety and efficacy of vaccines and drugs. Thus, the resources wasted on administration and on attempts to influence the adjudication committee would likely be small relative to the cost of developing a vaccine. Only companies that had actually developed a vaccine that had passed safety and efficacy tests would be able to apply for the program funds.

Plainly there is a continuum between the polar cases of vaccines and HIV counseling programs. Vaccines may be the technology where the need for commitments is greatest, and the difficulties of administration the smallest. Distortions are often more severe in markets for vaccines than in markets for drug treatments. Drugs have more vocal interest groups to lobby for their development and funding because the benefits of drugs are more concentrated. Since drugs are much more susceptible than vaccines to the spread of resistance, individual decisions to take drugs may create negative, as well as positive, externalities. Finally, as discussed in chapter 4, pharmaceutical manufacturers will typically find it easier to obtain revenue from consumers by selling drugs rather than vaccines.

Price guarantees could potentially be used to encourage drug R&D, but any program would have to address some additional challenges beyond those arising for vaccines. Regulators rarely, if ever, approve vaccines that have major side effects because vaccines are given to healthy people, many of whom would never get the disease in the absence of a vaccination program. This means that if a vaccine commitment requires regulatory approval, it need not specify in detail the rules regarding side effects. In contrast, since drugs are taken by sick people, regulators are often willing to approve drugs with significant side effects.

A drug with very dangerous side effects might not be worth taking to cope with an ordinary case of malaria, but might be appropriate to fight drug-resistant cerebral malaria. As a result, a purchase commitment for drugs would have to specify the purchase price associated with a particular group of side effects. The number of vaccine doses needed can be estimated from aggregate population data, whereas the number of drug doses needed depends on a multitude of decisions by individual patients and health-care providers.

As some drugs already exist for most diseases, a commitment for drugs would run the risk of creating a wasteful incentive to develop new therapies that are only slightly better than existing ones. Because drug resistance is more likely to develop than vaccine resistance, new drugs (for malaria or tuberculosis, for example) are sometimes restricted to patients who have strains of diseases resistant to mainstream treatment. Thus, a program providing a subsidy for new drugs could potentially cause a counterproductive shift toward their use. It seems likely that these problems could be addressed through careful program design, but these issues would have to be carefully thought through.

Advance guarantees could also potentially be used to encourage R&D on other products, like insecticides to fight malaria. A safe, environmentally benign insecticide might prove an excellent way to fight malaria, but it might be difficult to specify the conditions under which an insecticide would qualify for incentives. While environmental regulators are responsible for regulating pesticides, environmental regulatory systems are arguably generally less refined and are less insulated from political lobbying than medical regulatory systems. Specifying a pull program for an insecticide might therefore be more difficult than for either vaccines or drugs. This suggests that a greater emphasis on push programs might be appropriate for these technologies.

INCENTIVES FOR AGRICULTURAL R&D

The market for innovations in tropical agriculture faces many of the same problems as the market for vaccines, and is thus another area in which pull programs could have a major impact.[1] The R&D needed for tropical agriculture is distinct from that for temperate countries for numerous reasons, including differing types of staple crops, distinct agroecological systems, and ecospecific weeds and pests—all of which are part of a broader phenomenon in which agricultural technologies "spill-over" more easily within ecological zones than be-

---

[1] This section draws heavily on joint work with Alix Zwane, "Encouraging Technical Change in Tropical Agriculture" (2003).

tween them (Diamond 1997). But while agricultural R&D spending is 2.39 percent of agricultural GDP in developed countries, for sub-Saharan Africa it is only 0.58 percent. The situation is even worse for private agricultural R&D, of which virtually none is targeted towards low-income countries.

Like R&D on vaccines, research and development in tropical agriculture is a global public good, and is thus likely to be underproduced. A key market failure inhibiting developers from recovering the cost of R&D in agriculture is the potential for the resale of seeds. Plants and animals reproduce, and in developing countries farmers not only often reuse seed, but resell it in local markets. This drives down seed prices, making it more difficult for developers of new varieties to recoup R&D costs and thus reduces incentives for them to invest in tropical agriculture.

Many argue that researchers working under push programs produce seeds that are effective on experimental plots, but do poorly in real-world conditions and lack characteristics that farmers deem important. Diffusion of new technologies has sometimes been difficult in tropical agriculture (Christensen 1994; Carr 1989; IITA 2002; Santaniello 2002).

Rewards with pull programs in agriculture would therefore need to be linked to the acceptance of the technology by farmers. For example, developers of new seeds could be paid based on the number of hectares sown with their seed.

Under such a pull program, researchers would have strong incentives to maximize product adoption, and thus to make technological advances that take into account local ecologies and real-world farming practices. Innovators would also have incentives to accommodate the need to make new food crops taste and look good, and to work with national agricultural research systems to adapt seeds to local needs.

More broadly, purchase commitments or price guarantees could potentially be used to spur a wide variety of needed inventions. They could join other tools for stimulating research like the patent system and the peer review system. While the most tangible and immediate outcomes of a vaccine commitment would be the successful development of new vaccines, an additional outcome would be the development of a new tool for stimulating R&D.

Of course, it is likely to require time and experimentation to refine this new tool, just as it took time for institutions such as the patent system or the peer review process to evolve into their current forms. The institutions that today are integral in supporting our systems of innovation required both time and trial-and-error to develop. For example, the roots of the patent system extend back to medieval times with the grant of exclusive monopolies by sovereigns, often for products for which no R&D was required. Since the first U.S. Patent Act was put in place in 1790, rules have developed on what is allowed to be patented, who is allowed to file patents, for how long patents should be held, and so on.

An oft-cited historical example of the early roots of peer review is the story of Spanish physician Michael Servetus, who published a text suggesting that blood flows from one side of the heart to the other via the lungs. This idea contradicted the prominent theory of the time that was embraced as truth by the Catholic Church, and as the proposal of alternative hypotheses was heresy, Servetus was rewarded for his discovery of pulmonic circulation by being burned at the stake with a copy of his offending book strapped to his waist.

The peer review progress has certainly made tremendous progress since. Weller (2001) discusses how prior to World War II, editors of academic journals frequently made all decisions themselves with only informal advice from colleagues, and that only recently has the paradigmatic "editor plus two referees" system become widespread (Rowland 2002). Work by individuals such as Vannevar Bush, who lobbied for the evaluation of scientific research by scientists, not government officials, led to the establishment of the modern system of federally supported peer-review institutions for decision-making on federal funding for scientific research in the United States.

Like these other institutions designed to encourage innovation, a purchase commitment or price guarantee approach would need time and experimentation to evolve into an optimum design. The first step in developing these commitments as a tool for encouraging R&D would be to try the system in a few cases where current R&D incentives are inadequate and where the pull approach seems well suited to fill the gap.

■   ■   ■   ■

12. MOVING FORWARD WITH
VACCINE COMMITMENTS

A vaccine commitment has considerable appeal across the ideological spectrum as a market-oriented mechanism that brings the resources and inventiveness of the private sector to the fight against diseases disproportionately killing some of the world's poorest people. To move forward, it will be necessary for institutions with sufficient resources to launch a legally binding commitment program. Ideally, this would be structured in a way that encourages others to become cosponsors. Although vaccine commitments could be supported by multiple sponsors, due to the momentum needed for even one organization to overcome the bureaucratic and financial obstacles needed to support a vaccine commitment, the leadership of one organization would be needed. Following this, support from other organizations could fall into place more easily.

A host of policy leaders and organizations have endorsed the concept of vaccine commitments. The idea was discussed by the WHO (1996) and was advocated by a coalition of organizations coordinated by IAVI at the 1997 Denver Summit of industrialized countries. The 2001 report of the WHO Commission on Macroeconomics and Health recommended vaccine pull programs in the form of both purchase commitments and extensions of orphan drug laws (Commission on Macroeconomics and Health 2001).

In Britain, both Clare Short (the former Development Minister) and Gordon Brown (the Chancellor of the Exchequer) have endorsed vaccine commitments, and the UK Cabinet Office has also proposed an advance purchase commitment as part of a broader set of measures to fight communicable diseases (PIU 2001). Additionally, both Eveline Herfkens (Herfkens 1999), former development minister of the Netherlands, and Joschka Fischer, foreign minister of Germany, have endorsed the concept.

The Clinton administration proposed a pull program for HIV, tuberculosis, and malaria vaccines. Larry Summers, then Secretary of the Treasury, was a key advocate. Legislation incorporating these provisions was introduced in Congress by Senators Bill Frist and John Kerry, and by Representatives Nancy Pelosi and Jennifer Dunn. As of this writing, Kerry is the likely Democratic nominee for president, Senator Frist has since become the majority leader, and Representative Pelosi has become House minority whip, implying that vaccine pull initiatives may have influential advocates in both parties. An Institute of Medicine committee has also recommended pull programs for vaccines in the United States (IOM 2003). And as we will discuss, the Bush administration's Project Bioshield, intended to improve vaccines and drugs that protect against chemical and biological warfare, uses a spending authority intended to function as a pull program.

Making a Commitment Legally Binding

A key step in moving forward is to design a commitment with sufficient credibility to provide investors with the reassurance they need before investing millions of dollars in research. We have discussed elsewhere various essential elements for building credibility—for example, having an independent adjudicating committee that developers trust. Another key element, however, is establishing a legally binding contract. The historical and legal record provides strong evidence that a suitably designed commitment will be interpreted by the courts as a legally binding contract (Morantz and Sloane 2001).[1] Courts have ruled that publicly advertised contests are legally binding contracts, obligating sponsors to pay the winners according to their public announcements (Sullivan 1988). A contestant is judged to have formed a valid and binding contract with the promoter by perform-

[1] The discussion below is based on Morantz and Sloane (2001).

ing the act requested by the sponsor. Sullivan cites a number of examples in which attempts to escape liability by changing the rules after a contestant has performed the desired act are treated as breaches of contract. Vaccaro (1972) notes that advertisements with certain specifications (e.g., identification of good, definite quantity of good) for the purchase of goods at specified prices have also been found to be legally binding.

If the procedures in a contest stipulate the judge of the contest (the IAC in this case), decisions made by the judge are usually treated as final, if made in good faith. When the contest judge is an independent party, the courts almost universally hold the decision as final unless the decision was made in bad faith or the judges exceeded the authority specified in contest rules.

A particularly interesting precedent was set in the 1960s, when the U.S. government used a contract offering to purchase manganese ore to stimulate domestic production. As part of the Domestic Manganese Purchase Program, the General Services Administration (GSA), a U.S. federal executive agency, issued regulations offering to purchase, at guaranteed minimum prices, "manganese ores that met the specifications detailed in the applicable regulations." In *Himfar v. United States* (355 F.2d 606, Ct. Cl. 209 [1966]), the Federal Court of Claims enforced a unilateral contract under which the federal government agreed to purchase at the predetermined price all domestic manganese ore that met certain criteria specified in its contract. Morantz and Sloane (2001) note that this decision provides compelling evidence that a vaccine commitment would be readily enforced, even against the government.

Since legally binding contracts can be written, placing funds in escrow would not be necessary as long as the sponsor of a vaccine commitment had sufficient funds to meet its obligation. The credibility of a commitment thus turns on issues of specifying eligibility and pricing rules, and on procedures for adjudicating claims.

Some commentators have suggested that a sponsor might attempt to renege on a commitment even with a legally binding contract and that a developer would not be in a position to sue because of potentially negative public reaction. However, the public would be unlikely to condemn a vaccine developer for seeking redress from a sponsor that reneged on a commitment after a vaccine has been found to be effective by the regulatory authorities, the adjudicating committee has ruled in favor of the developer, and developing countries have said they want the vaccine and are prepared to provide a copayment.

THE POLITICS OF CREATING MARKETS FOR VACCINES AND DRUGS

One attractive feature of pull approaches is that they pay for results. While surveys suggest considerable skepticism about foreign aid among the public, they also suggest that this is due to doubts about its effectiveness (PIPA 2001). When asked what percent of U.S. foreign aid they believed ended up helping people who actually needed it, the median estimate was 10 percent (that is, that 90 percent of foreign aid never reaches those it is meant to help), and 58 percent of those surveyed said that they would be more supportive of foreign aid if they knew it was going to the people who really needed it rather than to wasteful bureaucracies and corrupt governments. A clear advantage of governments pledging foreign aid to a vaccine commitment is that the resources would only be spent if the actual results were obtained, and would require no outlays unless an acceptable vaccine was actually developed.

Despite widespread enthusiasm, no vaccine commitment has been put in place. This is in part because there is no ready-made political constituency with a strong interest in such a commitment. Administrators of foreign aid programs and government science agencies win bigger budgets and more influence from push programs than from programs that make government outlays an adjunct to private initiatives.

For their part, pharmaceutical firms may welcome vaccine commitments, but they benefit more immediately from incentives such as R&D tax credits. Pharmaceutical companies might be expected to be strong advocates for a vaccine commitment but, while they may welcome such a program, they are unlikely to spend political capital lobbying for it. This is partly because pull programs are open to all comers and therefore highly competitive. Established pharmaceutical companies would generally prefer to be given push funding or an

R&D tax credit (where they get paid whether or not they produce a product). Pharmaceutical companies are also reluctant to admit that their research priorities are at all influenced by the size of the potential market. While it may seem obvious that potential profits influence research (indeed, you could argue that managers have a fiduciary duty to ensure they are), pharmaceutical firms are worried about being cast as evil profiteers if they suggest a larger market will influence their behavior. Finally, even a vaccine commitment of several billion dollars would be small compared to the size of rich country markets, which means pull will not be the highest priority of pharmaceutical lobbyists. On the other hand, biotechnology companies are more enthusiastic about pull programs, partly because they are less likely to benefit from R&D tax credits. They are less concerned about public relations partly because they are less established, but they also have less lobbying power.

Arguably, some activist groups may gain more publicity by attacking pharmaceutical companies than by advocating better incentive systems for private developers. Given these issues, a vaccine commitment would need a political champion to move forward.

POTENTIAL SPONSORS OF NEW MARKETS FOR VACCINES AND DRUGS

Commitments to purchase vaccines could be undertaken by private foundations, governments of industrialized countries, multilateral institutions such as the World Bank, or by a combination thereof. Here, we offer ideas on how programs could be tailored to the needs of specific sponsors and how multiple organizations could work together as sponsors. In thinking about how a commitment initiative could be funded, keep in mind the key factors that make for an effective commitment. In particular, the commitment (and therefore the sponsor) must be highly credible, and must be able to meet its obligations if a vaccine is developed. Moreover, the commitment should be structured in ways that do not interfere with efforts to fight disease using existing technologies.

Private Foundations

Private foundations would be well suited to this task. Because they have greater continuity of leadership, foundations are apt to find it easier than governments to make credible commitments to future vaccine purchases. Foundations are also less vulnerable to the tug of conflicting interest groups. On the other hand, only a few would have the resources to take on a commitment for a complex disease such as HIV, tuberculosis, or malaria on their own.

U.S. law requires U.S. private foundations to spend at least 5 percent of their assets annually, which suggests a natural way that "push" and "pull" incentives for vaccine development could be combined. A foundation could spend 5 percent of its assets each year on grants to expand use of existing vaccines and to underwrite early-stage research in new vaccines. Meanwhile, the foundation could put its principal to use by pledging that if a vaccine were actually developed, it would purchase large quantities at remunerative prices and distribute the vaccine in low-income countries.

National Governments

National governments could also play a valuable role in financing a commitment to purchase new vaccines. An obvious candidate would be the United Kingdom, as the UK Cabinet Office has already proposed an advance purchase commitment as part of a set of measures to fight communicable diseases (PIU 2001).

The United States is another potential sponsor, and one possible precedent is Project Bioshield. Part of the George W. Bush administration's antiterror agenda, Project Bioshield is a plan to develop protection against biological and chemical warfare which includes methods for expediting R&D for medical countermeasures. It also sets aside on the order of $6 billion for improving vaccines and drugs for smallpox, anthrax, and botulinum toxin over the next ten years. This spending authority is intended to function as a pull program, since it increases the chances that the government will buy relevant treatments if they are developed. The Infectious Diseases Society of America has called for Bioshield to be applied to a wide array of infectious diseases, and the program may be extended to include pathogens such as Ebola and bubonic plague. However, a key weakness of the program is that the government is not committed to paying specific prices for specific new therapies, so developers still run the risk that, after the fact, the government will offer terms that do not cover risk-adjusted R&D costs.

The importance of pull mechanisms for vaccines, including purchase commitments, was also endorsed in a recent U.S. Institute of Medicine report (2003).

World Bank

The World Bank's subsidized loans (provided through the International Development Association) represents another potential channel for supporting pull. The standard modalities of World Bank lending would need to be modified, however, to meet the needs of a vaccine commitment. Most important, priorities for IDA loans are usually only set over a five-year time horizon and the Bank has, in the past, been reluctant to earmark specific sums for specific programs. Yet it may take ten years or more to develop new vaccines, and private investors may require a very specific commitment from sponsors to risk the large sums needed to develop vaccines.

Note, too, that IDA loans at below-market rates carry an implicit subsidy of roughly 60 percent. And since the bulk of the expense of purchasing the vaccine represents R&D costs, which are pure public goods, the 40 percent copayment implied by a 60 percent subsidy seems too high.

The best option would be for the Bank to legally bind itself to provide IDA loans to any member state that wanted to purchase the vaccine as long as a number of prespecified conditions—in particular, price and efficacy—were met.

Simply by making loans on IDA terms,[2] the Bank would be pro-

---

[2] IDA terms are a 10-year grace period, a 0 percent interest rate, and maturities of 35 or 40 years.

viding a large subsidy for the purchase of vaccines. It could further subsidize the loans (i.e., reduce recipient countries' copayment) by offsetting part of the vaccine purchase price through grants. Alternatively, other donors—either private foundations or governments—could make a commitment to "buy down" IDA loans used to purchase vaccine. In other words, they could give the member money to repay the loan—as was done in the case of Nigeria's polio eradication campaign.

One particularly attractive element of this buy-down approach is that governments or private foundations could deposit promissory notes with a World Bank trust fund now, but would not need to make payments until appropriate vaccines were developed and IDA loans were extended for purchases. In cases where national budgeting rules were amenable, the commitment might not count toward government outlays until the funds were drawn. The Bank and/or donors might also want to make commitments to subsidize the cost of administering the vaccine.

It is essential to give vaccine developers confidence that they will be able to recoup R&D costs. To provide the necessary assurances, IDA would need to make a commitment that, once an adequate vaccine is developed, any IDA-eligible country where a vaccination effort would be cost-effective would not suffer a reduction in IDA allocations for other projects. Otherwise, since countries are restricted in the value of IDA credits they can use in a single year, it is possible that countries would be reluctant to use their IDA funds to purchase vaccines at the World Bank's commitment price. Instead, they might attempt to buy the vaccine at a price that covers only manufacturing costs, and use scarce IDA credits for other projects.

Addressing Institutional Sponsors' Concerns

Earmarking

Earmarking future resources for a specific purpose is sometimes regarded as undesirable because it reduces the sponsor's flexibility to provide funds where they are needed most. The World Bank, for example, has resisted setting aside a specific percentage of future IDA loans for education because it is not clear now that education projects will be the most effective use of the funds in the future. They want the flexibility to make comparisons across all possible uses of funds in the future, and earmarking would constrain this. However, earmarking is plainly necessary in the case of stimulating vaccine R&D, since biotechnical and pharmaceutical firms would not be willing to invest at appropriate levels *now* without confidence that they would be able to recoup these investments in the future. To make an analogy, in general, it might not make sense for a household to constrain its choices on how to split its future budget between food, clothing, and shelter. But if the house needs a new roof and the family wants to hire a roofing contractor to replace the roof, they will need to commit in advance to pay the contractor when the work is finished. Similarly, it is necessary to commit now to pay potential vaccine developers in order to induce them to start work.

It is also worth noting that unlike a general policy of earmarking, the vaccine initiative would include conditions helping to ensure that the loans would be cost-effective if they were triggered. In particular, the commitment to provide the loans would be conditioned on the vaccine being effective and the disease being sufficiently prevalent to make vaccination worthwhile. The price would have been set in advance at a level that would be highly cost-effective in terms of lives saved per dollar spent. Finally, the commitment would be very specific and by its nature would, under virtually any foreseeable future scenario, be a high priority in the fight against global poverty. As demonstrated in chapter 9, under any realistic scenario, a vaccine purchased at the guaranteed price would represent one of the most cost-effective health interventions available and save more lives than almost any alternative use of the same amount of funds.

Avoiding Conflict with Current Priorities

Agencies that do not have the ability to credibly commit future funds may face a tradeoff between funding current priorities and tying up resources in a pull commitment. The Global Fund to Fight AIDS, Tuberculosis and Malaria, for example, may decide to spend money on mosquito nets now, rather than wait for a vaccine. However, for organizations such as private foundations that are not planning to spend down their assets; national governments that can raise tax revenue in the future; and the World Bank, which has assured revenue through repayments of previous IDA loans, there is no sense in which a commitment "ties up" funds. A vaccine commitment should be treated as expenditure in the year the funds are actually spent, and should be seen as competing with other uses of funds in that year.

Because money would change hands in a pull initiative only when a successful vaccine was developed, commitments to finance purchases of new vaccines would not interfere with other programs designed to tackle diseases using existing technologies. So, for example, the World Bank, the U.S. government, or the Gates Foundation could use this year's budgets to prevent the spread of AIDS, promote the use of bed nets against malaria-bearing mosquitoes, or increase coverage with existing vaccines, while making a commitment to use resources available in the future to buy a vaccine that has been proven effective against malaria. As discussed, spending on vaccines would save more lives than virtually any comparable expenditure.

The Program Would Be Poverty-Focused

Pledging credits to purchase vaccines for these three diseases would be tightly focused on the poorest countries. Eighty percent of the 2.3 million people who died of AIDS last year lived in sub-Saharan Africa, and almost 90 percent of malaria cases are in sub-Saharan Africa. Tuberculosis is concentrated in Africa and South Asia. Of those countries where the burden of the disease is sufficient to make widespread vaccination cost-effective, over 70 percent fall within the World Bank's low-income, IDA-eligible category. Within countries, the benefits of the program would also be well-targeted. Most medical interventions are used disproportionately by the better off, but compared to other medical interventions, vaccines are better at reaching the poor, as effective delivery is likely to extend further down the income spectrum than the delivery of other interventions.

Multiple Sponsors

A vaccine commitment could be supported by multiple sponsors. One institution could establish the basic infrastructure and make an initial pledge. Others could later make pledges of their own. The initial pledge could cover specific diseases or countries, and later pledges might be used to broaden the program. Some countries might be reluctant to make commitments to a vaccine program under another donor nation's control. So it might make sense to build in procedures for representation of multiple donors on decision-making bodies at the start, even if only one or two donors initially committed to the program.

Alternatively, a price guarantee approach would allow sufficient flexibility for each of several donors to accommodate its own needs. The flexible structure of the price guarantee model can be illustrated by considering a hypothetical example. Say a private foundation agrees that if someone provides a $2 copayment per person vaccinated, the foundation would top up the price by $10, to a total of $12. A national government could commit to provide half the copayment necessary to gain the support of the private foundation. From there, it is possible that another national government could agree to commit to top up the $12 to $15, but on the condition that the vaccine would be approved for use in that country. (The idea here is that in some cases it would be politically unfeasible to sponsor a vaccine that would not gain approval in the sponsoring country.) Potential developers would then know that they would be guaranteed $15 per person protected, or $12, if a vaccine is developed that would not pass regulatory guidelines in the second country. Clearly the price guarantee structure is flexible enough to allow for a variety of scenarios which could fit the needs of various donors.

Any of several organizations—including the World Bank, national governments, and private foundations such as the Bill & Melinda Gates Foundation—have the resources to create credible purchase commitments that would stimulate vaccine and drug research. This would not be an easy or riskless undertaking. But the potential problems are trivial compared to living with the status quo, in which millions die annually from diseases like malaria, tuberculosis, and HIV, while private research on vaccines against these diseases languishes.

By offering to buy vaccines against these diseases, provided they are developed, a sponsor could harness the energy and inventiveness that the private sector has shown in confronting diseases common in high-income countries. If such a commitment failed to induce the development of the needed products, no public funds would be spent. If it succeeded, millions of lives would be saved each year at remarkably low cost.

REFERENCES

Acemoglu, Daron, and Joshua Linn. (2003). "Market Size in Innovation: Theory and Evidence from the Pharmaceutical Industry." National Bureau of Economic Research (NBER) Working Paper #10038.

Adams, Gregor, et al. (2001). "Consensus Statement on Antiretroviral Treatment for AIDS in Poor Countries." Available online at http://www.hsph.harvard.edu/organizations/hai/overview/news_events/events/consensus.html.

Ainsworth, Martha, Amie Batson, and Sandra Rosenhouse. (1999). "Accelerating an AIDS Vaccine for Developing Countries: Issues and Options for the World Bank." Mimeo, World Bank.

Anderson, Jim. (1989). "Plague of Mismanagement Infects Federal Agency's Malaria Project." *The Scientist* 3(14): 1.

Assis, A.M.O. et al. (1998). "*Schistosoma mansoni* Infection and Nutritional Status in Schoolchildren: A Randomized, Double-Blind Trial in Northeastern Brazil." *American Journal of Clinincal Nutrition* 68: 1247–53.

Associated Press. (2003). "AIDS Vaccine Tested on Humans." October 3.

Attaran, Amir, and Lee Gillespie-White. (2001). "Do Patents for Antiretroviral Drugs Constrain Access to AIDS Treatment in Africa?" *Journal of the American Medical Association* 286(15): 1886–92.

Aventis Pasteur. (2004). "Group A and C Meningococcal Infections." Available online at http://www.aventispasteur.com.

Bailey, Britt. (2001). "Think You Own Your Genes? Think Again." *San Francisco Chronicle*, March 29.

Bainbridge, William Sims. (2003). "Privacy and Property on the Net: Research Questions." *Science* 302 (September): 1686–87.

Balke, Nathan S., and Robert J. Gordon. (1989). "The Estimation of Prewar Gross National Product: Methodology and New Evidence." *Journal of Political Economy* February (97): 38–92.

Barbaro, Michael. (2004). "FluMist Offered Free to Public Health Agencies." *Washington Post*, January 21: E01.

Barner, Klaus. (1997). "Paul Wolfskehl and the Wolfskehl Prize." *Notes of the American Mathematical Society* 44(10): 1294–1303.

Batson, Amie. (1998). "Win-Win Interactions Between the Public and Private Sectors." *Nature Medicine* 4 (Supp.): 487–91.

Becerra, Mercedes, et al. (2000). "Multidrug-Resistant Tuberculosis: The Challenge of Eliminating Disparities in Incidence, Treatment, and Outcomes." American Public Health Association 128th Annual Meeting, Abstract #13691.

Bergquist, Robert. (2004). "Prospects for Schistosomiasis Vaccine Development." UNICEF-UNDP-World Health Organization Special Programme for Research and Training in Tropical Diseases.

Berndt, Ernst, Pia Bruce, Michael Kremer, and Georg Weizsacker. (2003). "Estimating the Required Volume of a Malaria Vaccine Commitment." Mimeo, Harvard University.

Bernstein, J., and M. I. Nadiri. (1991). "Product Demand, Cost of Production, Spillovers, and the Social Rate of Return to R&D." NBER Working Paper #3625.

Bernstein, J., and M. I. Nadiri. (1988). "Interindustry R&D, Rates of Return, and Production in High-Tech Industries." *American Economic Review* 78: 429–34.

Bishai, D., M. Lin, et al. (1999). "The Global Demand for AIDS Vaccines." Presented at 2nd International Health Economics Association Meeting, Rotterdam, June 2.

Black, R. E., et al. (2003). "Child Survival II: How Many Child Deaths Can We Prevent This Year?" *Lancet* 362, July 5.

Bloland, Peter B. (2001). "Drug Resistance in Malaria." Geneva: World Health Organization (WHO).

Bojang, Kalifa, et al. (2001). "Efficacy of RTS,S/AS02 Malaria Vaccine Against Plasmodium *Falciparum* Infection in Semi-immune Adult Men in The Gambia: a Randomized Trial." *Lancet,* 358: 1927–34.

Borrus, Michael. (1992). "Investing on the Frontier: How the U.S. Can Reclaim High-Tech Leadership." *The American Prospect* 3(11): September 1.

Breman, J. G., A. Egan, and G. T. Keusch. (2001). "The Intolerable Burden of Malaria: a New Look at the Numbers." *American Journal of Tropical Medicine and Hygiene*, 64 (1–2 Supp.): iv–vii.

Brooks-Jackson, J., et al. (2003). "Intrapartum and Neonatal Single-Dose Nevirapine Compared with Zidovudine for Prevention of Mother-to-Child Transmission of HIV-1 in Kampala, Uganda: 18-month Follow-up of the HIVNET 012 Randomised Trial." *Lancet* 362: 859–67.

Brown, Geoffrey. (1990). "Aid Malaria Unit Acts to Regain Credibility as Probe Continues." *The Scientist* 4(5): 2.

Brown, Gordon. (2001). Speech given by Gordon Brown, Chancellor of the Exchequer, at the International Conference Against Child Poverty, London, February 26. Available online at http://www.hm-treasury.gov.uk/docs/2001/child_poverty/chxspeech.htm.

Carr, Stephen J. (1989). *Technology for Small-Scale Farmers in Sub-Saharan Africa: Experiences with Food Crop Production in Five Major Ecologic Zones.* Washington, D.C.: World Bank.

Centers for Disease Control. (2003). "Using Live, Attenuated Influenza Vaccination for Prevention and Control of Influenza." *Morbidity and Mortality Weekly Report* 52: RR13.

Centers for Disease Control. (2000). "Meningococcal Disease and College Students: Recommendations of the Advisory Committee on Immunization Practices." *MMWR Recommendations and Reports*, June 30: 11–20.

Centers for Disease Control. (1994). "Implementation of the Medicare Influenza Vaccination Benefit—United States, 1993." *Morbidity and Mortality Weekly Report* 43(42): 771–73.

Center for Global Development. (2004). "What's Worked: Accounting for Success in Global Health, Report of the What's Worked Working Group of the Global Health Policy Research Network." Washington, D.C.: Center for Global Development.

Center for Medicines Research International. (2001). "International Pharmaceutical R&D Expenditure and Sales 2001: Pharmaceutical Investment and Output Survey, Data Report I." Surrey, UK: Center for Medicines Research International.

Chaudhury, Nazmul, Jeff Hammer, Michael Kremer, Karthik Muraldhiran, and Halsey Rogers. (2004). "Teachers and Health Care Provider Absenteeism: A Multi-Country Study." World Bank. Unpublished.

Children's Vaccine Program. (2002). "The Case for Childhood Immunizations." Occasional Paper #5.

Chima, R., C. Goodman, and A. Mills. (2003). "The Economic Impact of Malaria in Africa: A Critical Review of the Evidence." *Health Policy* 63(1): 17–36.

Christensen, Cheryl. (1994). "Agricultural Research in Africa: A Review of USAID Strategies and Experience." *SD Publication Series*, Technical Paper No. 3. USAID Office of Sustainable Development, Bureau for Africa.

CNNfn. (1998). "Merck Slashes Zocor Price." May 1.

Cohen, Linda, and Roger Noll. (2001). *The Technology Pork Barrel*. Washington, D.C.: Brookings Institution.

Commission on Macroeconomics and Health (CMH). (2001). "Macroeconomics and Health: Investing for Health." Available online at http://www.cid.harvard.edu/cidcmh/CMHReport.pdf.

Connelly, Patrick. (2002). "The Cost of Treating HIV/AIDS with ARVs in South Africa: Who Knows? Who Cares?" Presented at the International AIDS Economics Network Symposium, Barcelona.

Coombe, C. (2000a). "Keeping the Education System Healthy: Managing the Impact of HIV/AIDS on Education in South Africa." *Current Issues in Comparative Education* 3(1). Available online at http://www.tc.columbia.edu/cice/articles/cc131.htm.

Coombe, C. (2000b). "Managing the Impact of HIV/AIDS on the Education Sector." University of Pretoria, Centre for the Study of AIDS. Available online at http://www.csa.za.org/filemanager/fileview/18/.

Crofton, John, Pierre Chaulet, and Dermot Maher. (2003). *Guidelines for the Management of Drug-Resistant Tuberculosis*. Geneva: WHO Global Tuberculosis Programme.

Das, Jishnu. (2000). "Do Patients Learn About Doctor Quality?: Theory and an Application to India." Manuscript, Harvard University.

Davies, Kevin. (2001). *Cracking the Genome: Inside the Race to Unlock Human DNA*. New York: Free Press.

De Cock, K. M., et al. (2000). "Prevention of Mother-to-Child HIV Transmission in Resource Poor Countries: Translating Research Into Policy and Practice." *Journal of the American Medical Association* 283: 1175–82.

Department for International Development (UK). (2000). "Shaping Globalisation to Benefit All—Better Health for the Poor and Global Public Goods." Speech by Clare Short, October 19. Available online at http://www.dfid.gov.uk/public/news/press_frame.html.

Desowitz, Robert S. (1997). *Who Gave Pinta to the Santa Maria? Torrid Diseases in a Temperate World*. New York: W.W. Norton.

Desowitz, Robert S. (1991). *The Malaria Capers: Tales of Parasites and People*. New York: W. W. Norton.

Diamond, Jared. (1997). *Guns, Germs, and Steel*. New York: W.W. Norton.

DiMasi, Joseph, et al. (2003). "The Price of Innovation: New Estimates of Drug Development Costs." *Journal of Health Economics* 22: 151–85.

DiMasi, Joseph, et al. (1991). "Cost of Innovation in the Pharmaceutical Industry." *Journal of Health Economics* 10(2): 107–42.

Dupuy, J. M., and L. Freidel. (1990). "Viewpoint: Lag between Discovery and Production of New Vaccines for the Developing World." *Lancet* 336: 733–34.

Economist. (2003a). "AIDS Vaccine: Better Luck Next Time." March 1.

Economist. (2003b). "Vaccines Against Bioterrorism: Who Will Build Our Biodefences?" February 1.

Economist. (2002). "Imitation v Inspiration." September 12.

Economist. (2001). "The Right to Good Ideas." June 21.

Elliott, Larry, and Mark Atkinson. (2001). "Fund to Beat Third World Disease." *Guardian*, February 23.

Falkman, Mary Ann. (1999). "Metal Cans Still Preserve, Protect, and Provide Convenience." *Packaging Digest*, November: 64.

Fauci, Anthony. (2003). "HIV and AIDS: 20 Years of Science." *Nature Medicine* 9(7): 839–44.

Financial Times. (2000). "Discovering Medicines for the Poor." February 2: 7.

Finkelstein, Amy. (2003). "Health Policy and Technological Change: Evidence From the Vaccine Industry." Mimeo, Harvard University.

Fogel, R.W. (2002). "Nutrition, Physiological Capital, and Economic Growth." Pan American Health Organization and Inter-American Development Bank. Available online at http://www.paho.org/English/HDP/HDD/fogel.pdf.

Galambos, Louis. (1995). *Networks of Innovation: Vaccine Development at Merck, Sharp & Dohme, and Mulford, 1895–1995*. Cambridge: Cambridge University Press.

Gallup, John, and Jeffery Sachs. (1998). "The Economic Burden of Malaria." Working Paper, Harvard Institute for International Development. Available online at http://www.hiid.harvard.edu.

Gingrich, Newt. (2002). "Dangle Prizes, Solutions Will Follow." *USA Today*, January 21.

Glennerster, Rachel, and Michael Kremer. (2001). "A Vaccine Purchase Commitment: Preliminary Cost-effectiveness Estimates and Pricing Guidelines." Unpublished.

Glennerster, Rachel, and Michael Kremer. (2000). "A World Bank Vaccine Commitment." Brookings Policy Brief 57.

Global Alliance for Vaccines and Immunization (GAVI). (2004). "Health, Immunization, and Economic Growth, Research Briefing #2, Vaccines are Cost-effective: A Summary of Recent Research." Available online at http://www.vaccinealliance.org.

Global Forum for Health Research. (2002). *The 10/90 Report on Health Research 2001–2002*. Geneva, Switzerland.

Global Health Council. (2003). "U.S. Coalition for Child Survival, State of Child Survival." Available online at http://www.child-survival.org/stateof.html.

Grabowski, Henry. (2003). "Increasing R&D Incentives for Neglected Diseases—Lessons from the Orphan Drug Act." Mimeo, Duke University.

Grabowski, Henry, John Vernon, and Joseph DiMasi. (2002). "Returns on R&B for New Drug Introductions in the 1990s." Duke University Department of Economics, working paper.

Griliches, Zvi. (1957). "Hybrid Corn: An Exploration in the Economics of Technological Change." *Econometrica* 25: 501–22.

Groseclose, Timothy. (2002). "GreenWorld and Energy Efficiency Standards." Mimeo, Stanford Graduate School of Business.

Guay, Laura A., et al. (1999). "Intrapartum and Neonatal Single-Dose Nevirapine Compared with Zidovudine for Prevention of Mother-to-Child Transmission of HIV-1 in Kampala, Uganda: HIVNET 012 Randomised Trial." *Lancet* 354 (9181): 795–802.

Guell, Robert C., and Marvin Fischbaum. (1995). "Toward Allocative Efficiency in the Prescription Drug Industry." *Milbank Quarterly* 73: 213–29.

Gupta, Rajesh, Alexander Irwin, Mario C. Raviglione, and Jim Yong Kim. (2004). "Scaling-up Treatment for HIV/AIDS: Lessons Learned from Multidrug-Resistant Tuberculosis." *Lancet* 363: 320–24.

Hall, Andrew J., et al. (1993). "Cost-effectiveness of Hepatitis B Vaccine in The Gambia." *Transactions of the Royal Society of Tropical Medicine and Hygiene* 87: 333–36.

Hall, Bronwyn. (1993). "R&D Tax Policy During the Eighties: Success or Failure?" *Tax Policy and the Economy* 7: 1–36.

Haseltine, William. (2001). "Beyond Chicken Soup." *Scientific American*, November.

Hayami, Yujiro, and Vernon Ruttan. (1971). *Agricultural Development: An International Perspective.* Baltimore: Johns Hopkins University Press.

Hayward, Andrew, and Richard Coker. (2000). "Could a Tuberculosis Epidemic Occur in London As It Did in New York?" U.S. Centers for Disease Control, *Emerging Infectious Diseases* 6(1).

Henkel, John. (1999). "Orphan Drug Law Matures Into Medical Mainstay." *FDA Consumer Magazine*, May-June. Available online at http://www.fda.gov/fdac/features/1999/399_orph.html.

Herfkens, Eveline. (1999). "Strategies for Increasing Access to Essential Drugs: The Need for Global Commitment." Presentation at the Conference for Increasing Access to Essential Drugs in a Globalised Economy, Amsterdam, The Netherlands, November 25–26.

Hilts, Philip. (1994). "U.S. Plans Deep Cuts in Malaria Vaccine Program." *New York Times*, February 13, p. 17.

Himfar, Albert W. v. United States. (1966). 355 F.2d 606; 174 Ct. Cl. 209.

Hoffman, Stephen L. (Ed.). (1996). *Malaria Vaccine Development: A Multi-immune Response Approach.* Washington, D.C.: American Society for Microbiology.

International Institute of Tropical Agriculture. (2002). *Annual Report.*

Jackson, J. Brooks, et al. (2003). "Intrapartum and Neonatal Single-dose Nevirapine Compared with Zidovudine for Prevention of Mother-to-child Transmission of HIV-1 in Kampala, Uganda: 18-month Follow-up of the HIVNET 012 Randomised Trial." *Lancet* 362(9387): 859–67.

Jaiswal, A., et al. (2003). "Adherence to Tuberculosis Treatment: Lessons from the Urban Setting of Delhi, India." *Tropical Medicine and International Health* 8(7): 625.

Jamison, Dean T., et al. (2001). "Cross-Country Variation in Mortality Decline, 1962–87: The Role of Country-Specific Technical Progress." Commission on Macroeconomics and Health Working Paper No. WG1:4, April. Available online at http://www.cmhealth.org/docs/wg1_paper4.pdf.

Jamison, Dean T., et al. (1993). *Disease Control Priorities in Developing Countries.* New York: Published for the World Bank [by] Oxford University Press.

Jha, P., et al. (2001). "Reducing HIV Transmission in Developing Countries." *Science* 292(5515): 224–25.

Johnston, Louis, and Samuel H. Williamson. (2002). "The Annual Real and Nominal GDP for the United States, 1789–Present." Economic History Services, April. Available online at http://www.eh.net/hmit/gdp/.

Johnston, Mark, and Richard Zeckhauser. (1991). "The Australian Pharmaceutical Subsidy Gambit: Transmitting Deadweight Loss and Oligopoly Rents to Consumer Surplus." NBER Working Paper #3783.

Jordan, William S., Jr. (1994). "Commission on Acute Respiratory Diseases Incorporating Three Other Commissions." In Theodore E. Woodward (ed.), *The Armed Forces Epidemiological Board: The Histories of the Commissions,* 63–67. Washington, D.C.: Borden Institute.

Jukes, M. C., et al. (2002). "Heavy Schistosomiasis Associated with Poor Short-Term Memory and Slower Reaction Times in Tanzanian Schoolchildren." *Tropical Medicine International Health* 7(2): 104–17.

Kakar, D. N. (1988). *Primary Health Care and Traditional Medical Practitioners.* New Delhi: Sterling Publishers.

Kamat V. R., and M. Nichter. (1998). "Pharmacies, Self-Medication and Pharmaceutical Marketing in Bombay, India." *Social Science and Medicine* 47(6): 779–94.

Katz, M. H., et al. (2002). "Impact of Highly Active Antriretroviral Treatment on HIV Seroincidence Among Men Who Have Sex With Men: San Francisco." *American Journal of Public Health* 92(3): 388–94.

Kelly, M. J. (2000). "Planning for Education in the Context of HIV/AIDS." Paris: UNESCO, International Institute for Educational Planning.

Kettler, Hannah E. (1999). "Updating the Cost of a New Chemical Entity." London: Office of Health Economics.

Kilbourne, Edwin D., and Nancy H. Arden. (1999). "Inactive Influenza Vaccines." In Stanley A. Plotkin and Walter A. Orenstein (eds.), *Vaccines, 3rd ed.* Philadelphia: W. B. Saunders.

Kim-Farley, R., and the Expanded Programme on Immunization Team. (1992). "Global Immunization." *Annual Review of Public Health* 13: 223–37.

Kremer, Michael. (2002). "Pharmaceuticals and the Developing World." *Journal of Economic Perspectives* 16(4): 67–90.

Kremer, Michael. (2001a). "Creating Markets for New Vaccines: Part I: Rationale." In Adam B. Jaffe, Josh Lerner, and Scott Stern (eds.), *Innovation Policy and the Economy, Vol. 1.* Cambridge: MIT Press.

Kremer, Michael. (2001b). "Creating Markets for New Vaccines: Part II: Design Issues." In Adam B. Jaffe, Josh Lerner, and Scott Stern (eds.), *Innovation Policy and the Economy, Vol. 1.* Cambridge: MIT Press.

Kremer, Michael. (1998). "Patent Buyouts: A Mechanism for Encouraging Innovation." *Quarterly Journal of Economics* 113(4): 1137–67.

Kremer, Michael, and Christopher Snyder. (2003). "Are Drugs More Profitable Than Vaccines?" NBER Working Paper #9833.

Kremer, Michael, and Alix Peterson Zwane. (2003). "Encouraging Technical Change in Tropical Agriculture." Unpublished.

Kurian, George Thomas. (1994). Datapedia of the United States 1790–2000. Lanham, MD: Bernan Press.

Lanjouw, Jean O. (1996). "The Introduction of Pharmaceutical Product Patents in India: 'Heartless Exploitation of the Poor and Suffering?'" NBER Working Paper #6366.

Lanjouw, Jean O., and Iain Cockburn. (2001). "New Pills for Poor People?: Empirical Evidence After GATT." *World Development* 29(2): 265–89.

Lichtmann, Douglas G. (1997). "Pricing Prozac: Why the Government Should Subsidize the Purchase of Patented Pharmaceuticals." *Harvard Journal of Law and Technology* 11(1): 123–39.

Malcolm, A., et al. (1998). "HIV-related Stigmatization and Discrimination: Its Forms and Contexts." *Critical Public Health* 8(4): 347–70.

Mansfield, Edwin, et al. (1977). *The Production and Application of New Industrial Technology*. New York: W. W. Norton.

Marseilles, E., et al. (1999). "Cost-Effectiveness of Single Dose Nevirapine Regimen for Mothers and Babies to Decrease Vertical HIV-1 Transmission in Sub-Saharan Africa." *Lancet* 354: 803–9.

McGarvey, S. T. (1992). "Nutritional Status and Child Growth in Schistosomiasis." *Rhode Island Medicine* 75(4): 187–90.

McGarvey, S. T., et al. (1996). "Schistosomiasis japonica and Childhood Nutritional Status in Northeastern Leyte, the Philippines: A Randomized Trial of Praziquantel versus Placebo." *American Journal of Tropical Medicine and Hygiene* 48(4): 547–53.

McNeil, Donald. (2004). "Plan to Bring Generic AIDS Drugs to Poor Nations." *New York Times*, April 6: F06.

McQuillan, Lawrence. (1999). "U.S. Vows to U.N. to Make Vaccines More Affordable." *USA Today*, September 22: 6A.

Mercer Management Consulting. (1998). "HIV Vaccine Industry Study October–December 1998." World Bank Task Force on Accelerating the Development of an HIV/AIDS Vaccine for Developing Countries.

Merck Pharmaceuticals. (1999). *Annual Report*.

Milstien, Julie B., and Amie Batson. (1994). "Accelerating Availability of New Vaccines: Role of the International Community." Global Programme for Vaccines and Immunization. Available online at http://www.who.int/gpv-supqual/accelavail.htm.

Mitchell, Violaine S., Nalini M. Philipose, and Jay P. Sanford. (1993). *The Children's Vaccine Initiative: Achieving the Vision*. Washington, D.C.: National Academy Press.

Moody's Investors Service. (2001). *Moody's Industrial Manual*.

Moorthy, Vasee, Michael Good, and Adrian Hill (2004). "Malaria Vaccine Developments." *Lancet* 363: 150–56.

Morantz, Alison, and Robert Sloane. (2001). "Vaccine Purchase Commitment Contract: Legal Strategies for Ensuring Enforcibility." Mimeo, Harvard University.

Mukherjee, Joia, et al. (2004). "Programmes and Principles in Treatment of Multidrug-Resistant Tuberculosis." *Lancet* 363: 474–81.

Muraskin, William A. (1995). *The War Against Hepatitis B: a History of the International Task Force on Hepatitis B Immunization*. Philadelphia: University of Pennsylvania Press.

Murray, Chirstopher J. L., et al. (2001). *The Global Burden of Disease 2000 Project: Aims, Methods, and Data Sources.* Geneva: WHO.

Murray, Christopher J. L., and Alan D. Lopez. (1996a). "The Global Burden of Disease: a Comprehensive Assessment of Mortality and Disability from Diseases, Injuries, and Risk Factors in 1990 and Projected to 2020." *Global Burden of Disease and Injury series, vol. 1.* Cambridge, MA: Harvard School of Public Health on behalf of the World Health Organization and the World Bank, Harvard University Press.

Murray, Christopher J. L., and Alan D. Lopez. (1996b). "Global Health Statistics: A Compendium of Incidence, Prevalence, and Mortality Estimates for Over 200 Conditions." *Global Burden of Disease and Injury Series, vol. 2.* Cambridge, MA: Harvard School of Public Health on behalf of the World Health Organization and the World Bank, Harvard University Press.

Nabel, G. J. (2001). "Challenges and Opportunities for Development of an AIDS Vaccine." *Nature* 410: 1002–7.

Nadiri, M. Ishaq. (1993). "Innovations and Technological Spillovers." NBER Working Paper #4423.

Nadiri, M. Ishaq, and Theofanis P. Mamuneas. (1994). "The Effects of Public Infrastructure and R&D Capital on the Cost Structure and Performance of US Manufacturing Industries." *Review of Economics and Statistics* 76: 22–37.

National Academy of Sciences. (1996). "Vaccines Against Malaria: Hope in a Gathering Storm." National Academy of Sciences Report. Available online at http://www.nap.edu.

National Institutes of Health. (2003). Office of Financial Management. Available online at http://www4.od.nih.gov/officeofbudget/FundingResearchAreas.htm.

Neumann, Peter J., Eileen Sandberg, Chaim A. Bell, Patricia W. Stone, and Richard H. Chapman. (2000). "Are Pharmaceuticals Cost-Effective? A Review of the Evidence." *Health Affairs*, March–April.

Nichter, Mark. (1982). "Vaccinations in the Third World: A Consideration of Community Demand." *Social Science and Medicine* 41(5): 617–32.

Nichter, Mark, and Mimi Nichter. (1996). *Anthropology and International Health: Asian Case Studies.* Amsterdam: Gordon and Breach.

Over, Mead, Peter Heywood, Sudhakar Kurapati, et al. (2003). "Integrating Antiretroviral Therapy and HIV Prevention in India: Costs and Consequences of Policy Options." Mimeo, World Bank PATH (Program for Appropriate Technology in Health). Available online at http://www.path.org.

Page-Shafer, K. A., et al. (1999). "Increases in Unsafe Sex and Rectal Gonorrhea Among Men Who Have Sex With Men—San Francisco, California, 1994–1997." *Morbidity and Mortality Weekly Report* 48(3): 45–48.

Paterson, D. L., S. Swindells, et al. (2000). "Adherence to Protease Inhibitor Therapy and Outcomes in Patients with HIV Infection." *Annals of Internal Medicine* 133(1): 21–30.

Pecoul, Bernard, Pierre Chirac, Patrice Trouiller, and Jacques Pinel. (1999). "Access to Essential Drugs in Poor Countries: A Lost Battle?" *Journal of the American Medical Association* 281(4): 361–67.

Pelosi, Nancy. (2000). "Pelosi Rises in Opposition to H.R. 2614- The Republican Tax Cut / BBA Giveback Package" [Floor Statement, U.S. House of Representatives]. October 26.

Performance and Innovation Unit, Cabinet Office (PIU). (2001). "Tackling the Diseases of Poverty: Meeting the Okinawa/Millenium Targets for HIV/AIDS, Tuberculosis, and Malaria." Available online at http://www.cabinet-office.gov.uk/innovation/healthreport/default.htm.

Phadke, Anant. (1998). *Drug Supply and Use: Towards a Rational Policy in India*. New Delhi: Sage Publications.

PhRMA. (2000a). PhRMA Industry Profile 2000. Available online at http://www.phrma.org/publications/publications/profile00/.

PhRMA. (2000b). PhRMA Annual Survey 2000. Available online at http://www.phrma.org/publications/industry/profile99/index.html.

PhRMA. (1999). PhRMA Industry Profile 1999. Available online at http://www.phrma.org/publications/publications/profile00/tof.phtml.

Program on International Policy Attitudes (PIPA). (2001). "Americans on Foreign Aid and Hunger: A Study of U.S. Public Attitudes." Available online at http://www.pipa.org/OnlineReports/BFW/toc.html.

Preston, Samuel H. (1975). "The Changing Relation between Mortality and Level of Economic Development." *Population Studies* 2: 231–48.

Program on International Policy Attitudes (PIPA). (2001). "Americans on Foreign Aid and Hunger: A Study of U.S. Public Attitudes." Available online at http://www.pipa.org/OnlineReports/BFW/toc.html.

Public Citizen. 2002. *America's Other Drug Problem: A Briefing Book on the Rx Drug Debate*. Washington, D.C.: Public Citizen.

Reiffen, David, and Michael Ward. (2002). "Generic Drug Industry Dynamics." Mimeo, University of Texas at Arlington.

Reuters. (2003a). "Roche Cuts AIDS Drug Price Following Protest." February 13. Available online at http://www.reuters.com.

Reuters. (2003b). "Pfizer Announces Potential Malaria Discovery." June 17. Available online at http://www.reuters.com.

Rhodes, Richard. (1988). *The Making of the Atomic Bomb*. New York: Simon & Schuster.

Robbins, Anthony, and Phyllis Freeman. (1988). "Obstacles to Developing Vaccines for the Third World." *Scientific American* (November): 126–33.

Robbins-Roth, Cynthia. (2000). *From Alchemy to IPO: The Business of Biotechnology*. Cambridge, MA: Perseus Publishing.

Rogerson, William P. (1994). "Economic Incentives and the Defense Procurement Process." *Journal of Economic Perspectives* 8(4): 65–90.

Rosenhouse, S. (1999). "Preliminary Ideas on Mechanisms to Accelerate the Development of an HIV/AIDS Vaccine for Developing Countries." Mimeo, World Bank.

Rosenthal, Meredith B., Ernst R. Berndt, Julie M. Donohue, Arnold E. Epstein, and Richard G. Frank. (2003). "Demand Effects of Recent Changes in Prescription Drug Promotion." In D. M. Cutler and A. M. Gardner (eds.), *Frontiers in Health Policy Research*, Volume 6. Cambridge, MA: NBER.

Rowland, Fytton. (2002). "The Peer Review Process." *Learned Publishing* 15: 247–58.

Russell, Philip K. (1998). "Mobilizing Political Will for the Development of a Safe, Effective and Affordable HIV Vaccine." NCIH Conference on Research in AIDS.

Russell, Philip K. (1997). "Economic Obstacles to the Optimal Utilization of an AIDS Vaccine." *Journal of the International Association of Physicians in AIDS Care*, September.

Russell, Philip K., et al. (1996). *Vaccines Against Malaria: Hope in a Gathering Storm*. Washington, D.C.: National Academy Press.

Sachs, Jeffrey. (1999). "Sachs on Development: Helping the World's Poorest." *Economist* 352(8132): 17–20.

Sachs, Jeffrey, and Michael Kremer. (1999). "A Cure for Indifference." *Financial Times*, May 5.

Salkever, David S., and Richard G. Frank. (1995). "Economic Issues in Vaccine Purchase Arrangements." NBER Working Paper #5248.

Sandahl, Linda, et al. (1996). "Process Evaluation of the Super Efficient Refrigerator Program." U.S. Department of Energy.

Santaniello, V. (2002). "Biotechnology and Traditional Breeding in Sub-Saharan Africa." In T. M. Swanson (ed.), (*Biotechnology, Agriculture, and the Developing World: The Distributional Implications of Technological Change*), pp. 230–46. Northampton: Edward Elgar Publishing, Inc.

Sazawal, S., and R. E. Black. (2003). "Effect of Pneumonia Case Management on Mortality in Neonates, Infants, and Children: A Meta-analysis of Community Based Trials." *Lancet* 3: 547–57.

Sazawal, S., and R. E. Black. (1992). "Meta-analysis of Intervention Trials on Case-Management of Pneumonia in Community Settings." *Lancet* 340: 528–33.

Schmookler, Jacob. (1966). *Innovation and Economic Growth*. Cambridge, MA: Harvard University Press.

Scotchmer, Suzanne. (1999). "On the Optimality of the Patent Renewal System." *RAND Journal of Economics*, Summer, 30(2): 181–96.

Scott Morton, Fiona M. (1999). "Entry Decisions in the Generic Pharmaceutical Industry." *RAND Journal of Economics* 30(3): 421–40.

Shavell, Steven, and Tanguy van Ypserle. (1998). "Rewards Versus Intellectual Property Rights." Mimeo, Harvard Law School.

Shepard, D. S., et al. (1991). "The Economic Cost of Malaria in Africa." *Tropical Medicine and Parasitology* 42: 199–203.

Shi, Ya Ping. (1999). "Immunogenicity and In Vitro Protective Efficacy of a Recombinant Multistage Plasmodium *Falciparum* Candidate Vaccine." *Proceedings of the National Academy of Science* 96: 1615–20.

Shulman, Sheila R., and Michael Manocchia. (1997). "The U.S. Orphan Drug Programme: 1983–1995." *Pharmacoeconomics* 12(3): 312–26.

Siebeck, W., R. Evenson, W. Lesser, and C. Primo Braga. (1990). "Strengthening Protection of Intellectual Property in Developing Countries: A Survey of the Literature." World Bank Discussion Paper 112, Washington D.C.

Silverstein, Ken. (1999). "Millions for Viagra, Pennies for Diseases of the Poor." *The Nation* 269(3): 13–19.

Simons, Eric. (2003). "1927: Charles Lindbergh Crosses the Atlantic, Solo." *TriValley Herald*, December 12.

SmithKline Beecham. (1999). *Annual Report*.

Sobel, Dava. (1995). *Longitude*. New York: Walker and Company.

Spier, Ray. (2002). "The History of the Peer-Review Process." *TRENDS in Biotechnology* 20(8): 357–58.

Stephenson, L. (1993). "The Impact of Schistosomiasis on Human Nutrition." *Parasitology* 107 (supplement): S107–23.

Stern, Scott (with J. Gans). (2000). "Incumbency and R&D Incentives: Licensing the Gale of Creative Destruction." *Journal of Economics and Management Strategy* 9(4): 485–511.

Sternberg, Steve. (2003). "Health Agencies, Drug Company Team to Fight Tuberculosis." *USA Today*, June 4.

StopTB Partnership. (2002). *Basic Facts on TB: Stop TB, Fight Poverty*. March.

Sullivan, Michael P. (1988). "Private Contests and Lotteries: Entrants' Rights and Remedies." *American Law Reports, ALR* 4th 64.

Suozzo, M., and S. Nadal. (1996). "Learning the Lessons of Market Transformation Programs." In *Proceedings of the 1996 Summer Study on Energy Efficiency in Buildings*, 2.195–2.206.

Targett, GAT. (Ed.). (1991). *Malaria: Waiting for the Vaccine. London School of Hygiene and Tropical Medicine First Annual Public Health Forum.* New York: John Wiley and Sons.

Taylor, Curtis R. (1995). "Digging for Golden Carrots: An Analysis of Research Tournaments." *American Economic Review* (September), 85: 872–90.

Thurman, Sandra. (2001). "Joining Forces to Fight HIV and AIDS." *The Washington Quarterly* 24(1): 191–96.

Towse, Adrian, and Hannah Kettler. (2003). "Advance Purchase Commitments to Tackle Diseases of Poverty: Lessons from Three Case Studies." Mimeo, Office of Health Economics.

UNAIDS. (2002a). *AIDS Epidemic Update.* December.

UNAIDS. (2002b). "Projected Population Structures with and without the AIDS Epidemic," South Africa and Botswana. Available online at http://www .unaids.org.

UNAIDS. (2000). *AIDS Epidemic Update.* December.

UNAIDS. (1999). *Prevention of HIV Transmission from Mother to Child: Strategic Options.* August.

UNAIDS. (1998). *AIDS Epidemic Update.* December.

UNAIDS. (1997). *HIV/AIDS in Zambia.*

UNICEF. (2004). "Diarrhoeal Disease, Progress to date." New York: UNICEF.

UNICEF. (2003). *UNICEF.* Available online at http://www.unicef.org.

United Nations. (2003). "Two Years After Historic UN Session on HIV/AIDS, New Reports Show Progress But Member Nations Fall Short of Goals" [Press release]. September 22.

USAID. (2002). "Preventing Mother-to-Child Transmission of HIV." 14th International AIDS Conference.

U.S. Census Bureau. (2003). "International Data Base, 1B/98-2." Available online at http://www.census.gov/ipc/www/idbnew.html.

U.S. Census Bureau. (2000). "International Data Base, Table 028: Age-Specific Fertility Rates and Selected Derived Measures." Available online at http:// www.census.gov/ipc/www/idbnew.html.

U.S. Congress. Senate. (1982). Hearing to Review Federal and State Expenditures for the Purchase of Children's Vaccines. Subcommittee on Investigations and General Oversight, Committee on Labor and Human Resources. July 22, Washington, D.C.

U.S. General Accounting Office. (1999). "Global Health: Factors Contributing to Low Vaccination Rates in Developing Countries."

U.S. Institute of Medicine. (2003). *Financing Vaccines in the 21st Century: Assuring Access and Availability.* Washington, D.C.: National Academy Press.

U.S. Institute of Medicine. (1991). Committee for the Study on Malaria Prevention and Control: Status Review and Alternative Strategies. *Malaria: Obstacles and Opportunities: a Report of the Committee for the Study on Malaria Prevention and Control: Status Review and Alternative Strategies, Division of International Health, Institute of Medicine*. Washington, D.C.: National Academy Press.

U.S. Institute of Medicine. (1986a). *New Vaccine Development: Establishing Priorities, Volume 2: Diseases of Importance in Developing Countries*. Washington, D.C.: National Academy Press.

U.S. Institute of Medicine. (1985). *New Vaccine Development: Establishing Priorities, Volume 1: Diseases of Importance in the United States*. Washington, D.C.: National Academy Press.

Utzinger, J., et al. (2000). "Oral Artemether for Prevention of Schistosoma mansoni Infection: Randomised Controlled Trial." *Lancet* 355(9212): 1320–25.

Vaccaro, Don F. (1972). "Advertisement Addressed to Public Relating to Sale or Purchase of Goods at Specified Price as an Offer the Acceptance of which Will Consummate a Contract." *American Law Reports, ALR* 3d 43.

Vernon, John, and Henry Grabowski. (2000). "The Distribution of Sales Revenues from Pharmaceutical Innovation." *PharmoEconomics* 18(1): 21–32.

Walley, J. D., M. A. Khan, J. N. Newall, and M. H. Khan. (2001). "Effectiveness of the Direct Observation Component of DOTS for Tuberculosis: A Randomised Controlled Trial in Pakistan." *Lancet* 357(9257): 664–69.

Wawer, M. J., et al. (2003). "HIV-1 Transmission per Coital Act, by Stage of HIV Infection in the HIV+ Index Partner, in Discordant Couples, Rakai, Uganda" [Abstract 40]. Boston: Tenth Conference on Retroviruses and Opportunistic Infections.

Wax, Emily. (2003). "A Generation Orphaned by AIDS." *Washington Post*, August 13.

Wellcome Trust. (1996). *An Audit of International Activity in Malaria Research*. Available online at http://www.wellcome.ac.uk/en/1/biosfginttrpiam.html.

Weller, A. C. (2001). *Editorial Peer Review: Its Strengths and Weaknesses*. Silver Spring, MD: American Society for Information Science and Technology.

World Bank. (2003). *World Development Indicators*. Available online at http://publications.worldbank.org/WDI/indicators.

World Bank. (2002). *Education and AIDS: A Window of Hope*. World Bank.

World Bank. (2001). *World Development Indicators*. Washington, D.C.: Oxford University Press.

World Bank. (2000). *World Development Indicators*. CD-ROM.

World Bank. (1999). *Confronting AIDS: Public Priorities in a Global Epidemic.* World Bank Policy Research Report. New York: Oxford University Press.

World Bank. (1998). *World Development Indicators.* CD-ROM.

World Bank. (1993a). *Disease Control Priorities in Developing Countries.* New York: Oxford Medical Publications, Oxford University Press for the World Bank.

World Bank. (1993b). *World Development Report 1993: Investing in Health.* Washington, D.C.: Oxford University Press.

World Bank AIDS Vaccine Task Force. (2000). "Accelerating an AIDS Vaccine for Developing Countries: Recommendations for the World Bank." February 28.

World Health Organization (WHO). (2004). "Polio Eradication Fact Sheet and FAQ." Geneva: WHO.

World Health Organization. (2003). "The 3 by 5 Initiative" [Fact Sheet 274]. Geneva: WHO.

World Health Organization. (2002a). *WHO Global Tuberculosis Control Report.* Geneva: WHO.

World Health Organization. (2002b). *World Heath Report 2002.* Geneva: WHO.

World Health Organization. (2002c). "Strategic Direction for Research: Schistosomiasis." Available online at http://www.who.int/tdr/diseases/schisto/files/direction.pdf.

World Health Organization. (2001). *World Health Report 2001.* Geneva: WHO.

World Health Organization. (2000a). *World Heath Report 2000.* Geneva: WHO.

World Health Organization. (2000b). "Global Tuberculosis Control 2000." Available online at http://www.who.int/gtb/publications/globrep00/download.html.

World Health Organization. (2000c). *Anti-Tuberculosis Drug Resistance in the World—Report No. 2.* Available online at http://www.who.int/gtb/publications/dritw/index.htm.

World Health Organization. (2000d). "Less-Used Vaccines against Major Diseases Are Cost-Effective, Researchers Conclude." *Bulletin of the World Health Organization* 78(2): 274.

World Health Organization. (1999a). *World Heath Report 1999.* Geneva: WHO.

World Health Organization. (1999b). "Infectious Diseases: WHO Calls for Action on Microbes." June 17.

World Health Organization. (1999c). "Meningococcal and Pneumococcal Information Page." Available online at http://www.who.int/gpv-dvacc/research/mening.html.

World Health Organization. (1999d). *Issues Relating to the Use of BCG in Immunization Programmes*. Authors: Paul E. M. Fine, et al. Geneva: WHO.

World Health Organization. (1997a). *Weekly Epidemiological Report* 72: 36–38.

World Health Organization. (1997b). *Anti-Tuberculosis Drug Resistance in the World*. Geneva: WHO.

World Health Organization. (1997c). "World Malaria Situation in 1994, Part I." WHO *Weekly Epidemiological Record* 36: 269–74.

World Health Organization. (1996a). *Investing in Health Research and Development: Report of the Ad Hoc Committee on Health Research Relating to Future Intervention Options*. Geneva: WHO.

World Health Organization. (1996b). *World Health Organization Fact Sheet N94 (revised)*. Geneva: WHO.

World Health Organization and UNICEF. (1996). *State of the World's Vaccines and Immunization*. WHO/GPV/96.04. Available online at http://www.who.int/gpv-documents/docspf/www9532.pdf.

World Health Organization Regional Office for South-East Asia. (2002). "Prevention of Hepatitis B in India: An Overview." New Delhi, August.

World Trade Organization. (2001a). "Fact Sheet: TRIPS and Pharmaceutical Patents." April.

World Trade Organization. (2001b). "Declaration on the TRIPS Agreement and Public Health." Available online at http://www-chil.wto-ministerial.org/english/thewto_e/minist_e/min01_e/min01_14nov_e.htm.

Wright, Brian D. (1983). "The Economics of Invention Incentives: Patents, Prizes, and Research Contracts." *American Economic Review* (September), 73: 691–70.

INDEX

9 780691 171166